Love, Intimacy & Sex in the Second Half

Kim Kimberling, PhD
Nancy Kimberling

I0895692

Love, Intimacy, and Sex in the Second Half of Marriage
Kim Kimberling, PhD and Nancy Kimberling

www.loveinthesecondhalfbook.com

Published by The Core Media Group, Inc., www.thecoremediagroup.com.
The authors are represented by WordServe Literary Group, Ltd., www.wordserveliterary.com.

Cover & Interior Design: Nadia Guy

Top front cover photo: Harris Johnson Photography, Houston, TX
Bottom front cover/back cover photos: KGC Photography, Oklahoma City, OK

ISBN 978-1-950465-86-6

Printed in the United States of America.

Dedication

To our amazing God, who demonstrates love to us every day; who, through Jesus, teaches us about intimacy; and who gave us the incredible gift of sex in marriage.

Table of Contents

Introduction

If marriage were a football game, and every game lasted 50 years, then the second half of marriage would start on the twenty-fifth anniversary. If most of those couples were around 25 when they married, their second half would begin after their fiftieth birthdays. If marriages were that uniform, I could target married couples over 50 years old and be right on the mark. They would all be in the same stage of life. They would all have experienced ups and downs in their married life. They would all be in the second half of their marriage.

The major problem with this theory is that, in reality, no two marriages are the same. The scenario I just described probably encompasses 10 percent of the married population—or less. Tom and Denise got married when they were both 35. Matt and Carol married when Matt was 45 and Carol was 33. Alan and Mary married at 66, a few years after each lost their spouse. When the second half of marriage begins is unique to the individual couple. The second half for one couple may look very different from another couple.

My guess is that if you picked up this book, it's because you think you are, or may be, in the second half of your marriage. The person standing next to you in the bookstore who also picked up this book may look very different from you but also thinks that they are in the second half of their marriage.

For Nancy and me, the second half of marriage began when the final child left home and we were in our forties. Our married life to that point consisted of five years of marriage before kids and 20 years of marriage raising kids. Now we were entering a new season without kids at home. No longer did we have to be home to help with homework, to put kids to bed, or to make sure everyone was fed. We had a new freedom. The question before us was this: What do we want this new season to look like? We saw other couples enter this season and disconnect. We definitely did not want that.

We wanted our love to grow. We wanted to be passionate about each other and the life that was before us. We wanted our sex life to be better than ever. We knew it would not happen by accident. It would take focus, intentionality, and work. But the picture we had of what our marriage could be seemed more than worth all of the effort.

Our road has not been perfect. We made some mistakes and were not always on the same page. There were bumps in the road—some we expected and some we did not. Yet, with God's help, we have leveled out into a second half of marriage that we both cherish. We want to share our story with you and introduce you to some other couples living in their second half. Love, intimacy, and sex can thrive in the second half of marriage. Are you ready? The umpire just blew his whistle. It's time for the second-half kickoff. Let's go!

Part One

Love

Reasons Why

On your wedding day, if I had asked you why you loved your bride or groom, what would you have said? You may not remember! I loved Nancy because she was beautiful, fun to be with, and I could not wait to spend every night with her sleeping by my side. All three of those are still true today and I could add a fairly long list of other "reasons why."

She cares deeply for me. She anticipates what I need and want. She is the best best friend I have ever had. She puts up with me. She laughs when my jokes are funny—and when they are not. She lets her love for me win out over the anger she may feel toward me at times. She is willing to give anything a try—which is why hiking and pickleball have recently been added to our activity list. She takes me with her to get pedicures and pays for me to have one too. There are a lot more "reasons why," but I'll stop here and let Nancy share some of hers.

Nancy: When I first met you, it was an attraction. It wasn't really love. The love really didn't start happening until I started getting to know you better and better. But I thought I was in love until I got to be much older. Then I realized I didn't even know what love was really all about. When you go through seasons of your life, good and bad, and you learn to live with this other person that God's given you, then you learn to truly love them for who they are and what they mean to you. That deepens as you get older, until now I can say that I truly love you with everything, with my heart. And I couldn't say that even 10, 15, 20 years ago.

Dr. Kim: What are some specific reasons why?

Nancy: For all we've been through. I saw you mature into a young man, and now into a wise older gentleman that I can respect for who you are and what you've become. I don't think I really respected you when we first met. I knew you were a good guy, but I didn't have a lot to go on. Now that I've watched you live life and go through business and ministry, parenthood and grandparenthood, your counseling and your passion for marriage, and the respect others have for you, all of that has deepened my respect for you.

Questions for You:

- What would you have said on your wedding day if I had asked you why you loved your spouse?
- What are some reasons you love your spouse today that you can add to your list?

One of the prayers that I have seen God answer for me is to grow and deepen my love for Nancy. I really do not think my love for her would have grown the way it has without God's help. I often ask Him to help me see Nancy through His eyes. Wow, that has made a big difference. He strips away my critical spirit and selfishness and helps me embrace her as the gift He has given me in this marriage. I don't think that love ever has to stop growing in a marriage, but it can fizzle out if we let it. We have to make the choice: Will our love grow or will it fizzle?

I have always been a perfectionist of sorts. There are some people who know me pretty well who would say, "Not 'of sorts.' You are a perfectionist—period." Being a perfectionist has its pros and cons. In my work, it pays off. I want to do everything with excellence, whether in the counseling room or leading Awesome Marriage. It becomes a con when I bring that drive for perfection to more intangible things, like marriage. Do I want a perfect marriage? Yes. Is that even possible? No. Expecting a marriage to be perfect is an impossible expectation and a set-up for deep disappointment.

Either consciously or subconsciously, I went into marriage with a plan. My plan was to figure it out, communicate it well to Nancy, and have this whole "perfect marriage" thing nailed down for a lifetime. I wanted to get it nailed down and then never have to work on it anymore. I worked really hard at it for a long time. There were two problems. First, I was not prayerful about my plan. It was my plan without any input from God. Second, I was one person making a plan for two people and I left Nancy out of the process. She was not really on board with my plan for our marriage. She had her own ideas about what our marriage needed to be.

What we really needed was, with God's help, to develop our plan together instead of having separate plans that were in competition with each other. Yet there was one thing about my plan that made sense and was worth salvaging. Having a plan was actually a good idea. The plan needed one change: The plan for our marriage had to be God's plan, not mine. His plan for marriage is about serving our spouse, not having them serve us. It's about embracing their differences instead of trying to change them. It's about being unselfish and forgiving. It's about putting Him first and seeking His guidance and wisdom.

I began to view marriage as a highway. The highway begins with "I dos" at the altar and ends after a lifetime together. Along that highway are bumps and potholes, which are the tough situations we all have to navigate at some point over the course of our marriage. Then there are detours and exits, the things that can take us away from our marriage. (Those are never a good idea.) The goal of a marriage is to stay on the highway and stay focused on the route toward an awesome marriage. Everything I do each day needs to be toward that goal. If it isn't, then the bumps, potholes, detours, and exits come into play. Sometimes they come into play anyway. But if I stay focused on the goal, I can recover and get back on a nice, smooth highway.

Love grows as we ride along the highway if the right One is driving the car. When we let Him drive the car, we are much safer, and He has the perfect plan for our marriage. When Nancy or I drive the car, we are much more likely to encounter a road hazard. Our selfishness kicks in. We are not serving each other. We fight to get our own way instead of working together. When we let God drive the car, things are so much different. We let Him be in control. We acknowledge that His plan for our marriage is much, much better than anything we could come up with on our own. We focus on each other. We both focus on Him. When we focus on Him, the distractions don't seem so overwhelming, and we can deal with them. All of that lays the foundation for our love for each other to grow, and grow it does.

Dr. Kim: I think that in the early years of our marriage, I wanted Nancy to love me more than I loved her. It gave me some type of false security. It made me feel more in control. It made me think that she would never leave me. So I worked hard at keeping the imbalance in place. The truth was that I was holding back. I did not want to get hurt, so I put up an invisible wall to protect myself. It is interesting how we can think things that are so completely ridiculous and unhealthy are working. I finally realized I was missing out on what I really desired to have in my marriage: love. Love that grows and grows and grows. Love that is willing to risk all. Love as God intended it to be in marriage.

Nancy: I can look back on that and realize I loved you with was an insecure type of love. I needed you to be a provider, a father. My love was more a reliance on you and what you could do rather than just loving who you were as a man and a person. At this point in our marriage, my love has grown through all the things we've been through. Part of that was me being an anxious person. You were so patient with me through that, and through a major depression. That deepened my love for you. I learned to understand how to receive pure *agape* love. Not a sexual love, or something that was more like infatuation, but a more mature love. I knew you really loved me, and I knew what that love meant, and that changed my life.

Questions for You:

- How would you describe the love for your spouse in the early years of your marriage?
- Have you ever held back to protect your heart?
- How would you rate your love in your marriage today on a 1 to 10 scale, with 10 being amazing?
- How would you describe God's perfect plan for love in a marriage?

Milestones

Dr. Kim: As I look back over our marriage, there were definitely milestones that took the love in our marriage to a new level. Most of the time we were able to keep the ground we gained and use it as a springboard to the next level. It's important for us to remember those significant times in our marriage that drew us closer to each other. For us, there were the times of warmth that we experienced with the birth of both of our children. We were five years into our marriage when Grant was born and we were more than ready to be parents. Then there was the joy of having a girl when Julie was born. We experienced fun times together that have added to our foundation and given us a lot of great memories.

For our twenty-fifth anniversary, we took a trip to the Caribbean. It was one of those magical trips that we really needed even though we didn't know we really needed it. Perfect weather. Perfect beach. Beautiful water. Amazing sunsets. We weren't quite empty nesters, but we were getting close. We spent every day and night together for a week. After spending so much time raising kids and filling our lives with all kinds of distractions, we got reacquainted. That may sound strange because we had a good marriage before the trip. But after that trip, we had a whole new focus for our marriage and the years in front of us. There are times in a marriage when we need a reset. It was one of those times for us and became a milestone moment.

Nancy: Looking back, there are definitely highlights. I think you grow with every season of life—every hour, every month. We've always had great friends and enjoyed doing things with friends we loved and respected. We enjoyed trips we'd take with family. For the two of us, our anniversary trip was truly a remarkable experience because we'd never really had anything like that. You know, we had our honeymoon, and that's when you're supposed to be romantic, but that had really failed me. On our honeymoon I was just miserable! I got sick, and I didn't want to be where we were. You were being bossy to me, and that made me push away from you a little bit. It was like I felt smothered. But we were just kids then!

That anniversary trip awakened a new part of us in a sexual way. Just being in a romantic place where we had nothing else to do but be together really pointed us in a new direction. After that trip, we really looked forward to going away by ourselves more after that and we made the time for it.

Another milestone I want to mention is about 10 years ago, when I quit drinking. I feel like I grew in love with you then. Before that, when we would have wine, that kind of blurred things. When you're drinking, not even getting drunk, but just drinking some, you feel more in love with everybody! So when I quit, that forced me to deal with what I was really feeling daily: anger, happiness, joy, romance.

Questions for You:

- When was the last time the two of you took a trip just for two? No family. No friends. Just you two. As you look to part two of your marriage, a trip might be the perfect way to start it off. Here are some thoughts:
- Think about a trip that gives you a lot of face-to-face time together. Beach trips are great for that. Don't do a trip where you think you have to tour everything and then hit the bed exhausted every night.
- If you can swing a week or more, go for it. It may take a day or two to unwind and get your focus set on each other.
- Talk. If this has been a regular part of your marriage, it should come pretty easy. If not, I promise you can do it. Get to know each other again.
- Keep your expectations realistic. Your goal is simple: to connect in a way that grows your love for each other.

I get emotional every time I think of two of our milestone moments. Both were crisis times when Nancy was sick and I was not sure if she would make it. Obviously, she did, but those two times made me stop and think about how much I loved her and how empty my life would be without her. God used those times to help me value our love and every day that we have together. It helped me realize that I was spending a lot of time not embracing that love and not cherishing my wife. They were wakeup calls that took my love for her to a new level.

One of our milestones was in the summer of 1986. That was a big year for us. Nancy and I were asked to go with a group of Christian counselors to Amsterdam to counsel itinerant evangelists attending a Billy Graham conference. We were really excited. Neither of us had been to Europe and the thought of serving at a Billy Graham event was awesome.

In the months before the trip, Nancy had been having some abdominal pain. She'd suffered from endometriosis since she was a teenager. There were good months and bad months. A few years earlier, a doctor we really trusted had encouraged her to consider surgery but we had two young kids and a busy life, so she kept putting it off. I went with her to a consultation appointment with a doctor she was seeing that I had not yet met. I liked him a lot but he was emphatic that surgery was needed and should not be put off any longer. We were to leave for Amsterdam in the middle of July and Nancy promised him she would have the surgery in August after we returned. He really wanted to do the surgery before we left but he found the same problem I dealt with all the time: Nancy is very hard to deal with when her mind is made up. So August it was!

Amsterdam was great. The conference was an eye-opening and encouraging experience for us. We also visited Belgium and London before returning home. On the final leg of our flight home, the reality of the upcoming surgery set in. A week later, we were at the hospital before the sun came up. It was surgery day. Nancy was nervous and it showed on the outside. I was nervous and held it on the inside. My parents were keeping our kids. I don't sit down when I am nervous, so for the two-plus hours of the surgery I paced.

Finally, a call came from recovery telling me she was fine and that the doctor would be out to talk to me in a few minutes. He said, "The surgery went well but it was difficult. She will be out of it for a while and very sore." I made the usual calls to family and friends and parked myself in her hospital room to wait for them to bring her up. Nancy was asleep and barely woke up when they moved her from the gurney to the bed. The nurses surrounded her and asked me to leave while they got her situated. I never quite understood that since she was my wife. It wasn't like they were going to uncover a part of her body that I had not seen! She slept most of that day and when she did wake up, she said some pretty funny things with the aid of a morphine drip.

The next week was a whirlwind. The kids continued to stay with my parents. I would stay at the hospital all day until they would suggest that I leave late at night. Each night, I drove the two miles home from the hospital. Each night as I walked upstairs to bed, I felt a heat wave when I reached the second story and I'd realize that I once again had forgotten to make a service call to get our broken upstairs AC unit repaired. Sleep was not easy anyway but the hot bedroom made it more difficult.

At the hospital, instead of looking better each day, Nancy looked worse. She was down to 108 pounds and was not much wider than the IV pole she was hooked up to. Her stomach was a different story. She looked pregnant. I kept asking questions. Something was not right. Finally, as I was leaving her room one night to go home, a nurse called me over. She was worried too. She told me that another woman six months earlier had the same reactions after the same surgery. When I asked what happened to that woman, the nurse looked me in the eyes and said, "She died."

That night I didn't sleep a bit. At six o'clock, I called a good family friend who was one of the best surgeons in the state. He met me at the hospital an hour later. By noon that day, Nancy was back in surgery with the original doctor and a specialist. I remember kissing her as they wheeled her out of the room, wondering if I would see her again. I went to the chapel, sat, and prayed.

An hour later, a nurse came in to say the doctors were finishing up and would probably be out soon. Just as I got to the waiting room, the doors to the surgery area opened and there came the two doctors. As a counselor, I am always looking for visual cues, so my eyes were fixed on both of them. Then I saw it: they were both smiling. The surgery was successful. Whatever was wrong was an easy fix. Nancy would be okay. We spent a total of 17 days in the hospital. The day before I brought her home, I finally got the air conditioner fixed. I never felt closer to her than during that time of crisis. God used it to show me how much I loved her and how precious each day is that He gives us together. My love went to a new depth then. Our marriage went to a new level.

Nancy: Any time you have a medical condition—like my surgery, your cancer surgery, my heart attack, or a bout of depression like we both went through—those times really can draw you closer. In those crises, you really were considerate. I could tell you really loved me and cared about me. That made a big impact on me. I don't think I grew up knowing what love really was—certainly not in a husband and wife sense. When I was growing up I would just dream of how I would be when I was married and had kids, that my husband would be so in love with me. And it happened! After all of that, I realized that dream was what I've got.

When you had your bout with prostate cancer, I was obviously worried and scared. Yet through that the Lord comforted me and I felt assured that you would be okay. I don't think I was prepared for the side effects of it afterward. We had to work together to get you to the point where you could have sex again or you would not be able to function. That was part of me learning to be patient. I could recall how you'd been patient with me in the past with problems I'd had, and that gave me an example.

I think we have a unique experience. I think we got married young, and we gutted it out and stayed committed to one another. I think that's what hanging in there and giving it your all can do, because now we're in a relationship that I would go back and do all over again if I had to.

Questions for You:

- Has there been a crisis time in your marriage that God used to grow your love?
- What did God teach you during that time?
- When you think back on that time, what emotions do you feel?

Looking Forward

To decide where we need to go and what we need to do, it is usually important to look at where we have been. I wanted you to remember those early days of marriage and the love you felt then. I wanted you to think about the way your love has grown over time and the milestones that marked the way. Now let's look at what lies ahead.

Questions for You:

- What will love in part two of your marriage look like?
- What do you want it to look like?
- What could get in the way of your love growing?
- What do each of you need to take responsibility for?
- What does God have in store for the two of you?

What Does It Look Like?

What does love look like in this second half of marriage? I used to be afraid that it meant sitting side by side in rocking chairs on a front porch, staring out at the world. Maybe that will be us one day, but I want the gap between today and that day to be very different. Today I want us to spend as much time together as possible. We are both really active and both are still working.

Since we both love what we do, I don't see that changing. We do have more time that we can use to be intentional about our marriage.

The definition of "love" as a noun goes something like this: "an intense feeling of deep affection." The synonyms are "fondness," "tenderness," "warmth," and "intimacy." The definition we will use for "love" as a verb is "to feel a deep affection for someone." The synonyms are "to cherish," "to treasure," or "to prize." "Love" as a noun is the feeling, and "love" as a verb is the action.

For me, it is a cycle. I love Nancy. It is that feeling deep within me. As I show her love through my actions and she receives my love, the feeling within me grows and I show my love through more actions, and on and on and on. That cycle has probably been going on for our entire marriage.

Let's take a detour to look at something that can ruin the cycle: wrenches. Wrenches are things we can throw right into the middle of the cycle that are 100 percent avoidable but that disrupt everything. Why would we disrupt this beautiful cycle by throwing a wrench in it, especially when we could have completely avoided it? Now that it has been thrown, what do we do? The solution is to deal with the wrench and get the good cycle going again.

I'm not sure how many wrenches I had at the beginning of our marriage, but there were a lot—probably more than I would ever want to sit down and count. Today there are probably a few left. It's not that I threw them all at our healthy marriage cycle, though I did throw a number of them. No, instead of throwing them at my marriage, I decided to throw them away. Far away.

In the next section I'm going to unpack three major wrenches for you to identify and throw away for the sake of a healthy marriage. Wrenches thrown at your marriage are destructive and cause a lot more work than they are worth. Whatever payoff they gave you in the moment wasn't worth it. I may still have a few wrenches left but my goal is to leave them in the first half of our marriage and not bring any into the second half. When I stand back and let the love cycle work, our marriage is really good.

Questions for You:

- How does the love cycle work in your marriage?
- What wrenches do you have that disrupt the cycle?
- What would it take for you to leave those wrenches behind as you enter into the second half of your marriage?

Three Killer Wrenches

Sometimes our wrenches have become such a part of our lives that we do not realize that we are still carrying them or the damage they can do. As long as we carry them there is still the chance that we might throw them. A wrench thrown can be a marriage killer. The marriage may not actually end, but it will never reach the potential that God intended it to reach. I want us to look at three of these wrenches that will harm the second half of your marriage if you do not leave them behind.

1. Information

By the time Nancy and I got married, we knew each other pretty well. We spent a lot of time together while dating. At the end of 10 years of marriage, we knew each other even better. Our knowledge of each other exponentially increased year after year. There are so many benefits to being a student of your spouse and knowing them better and better year after year. The more I learned about Nancy, the better I could serve her, love her, and make her life better. I learned what she liked and did not like. I learned what made her feel safe and secure. I learned what it took to be the husband she wanted and needed.

I also learned some other things as I knew her better and better. I learned what irritated her. I learned her weaknesses and fears. I learned how to win fights. I learned how to manipulate her. I acquired an arsenal of information that I could selfishly weaponize to get my way. There was power in this knowledge that I should never use in a selfish way. If a couple is to experience all that God has for them in their marriage, they have to take risks. They have to be willing to be transparent and vulnerable with each other. They have to trust at a level they have never trusted before.

When Nancy let me know her at the deepest levels, it was a sacred trust she put in me. She trusted me to never use this knowledge to hurt her in any way. Honestly, there were a few times I broke this trust. I hated the results. She put a wall of protection up and it took a lot of time and effort for her to let that wall down and trust at a deep level again.

Nancy: I certainly did this a lot early on. I weaponized your mother. She was so supportive of me, so when you would say or do something I didn't like, I would call her. One time you didn't want to take me somewhere and I called her about it. Then she called you and said, "Take her!" I basically tattled on you. But that was so early on; we were just kids.

I think later on, I did use some things I knew would bug you when we were out with other people. You never wanted other people to see the bad side of our relationship, and I'd deliberately sabotage that. I would just say something like, "I'm really mad at him." And I'd threaten you with it—like if we were at dinner or a party with friends, I'd threaten to tell them what you'd said to me when you were angry.

Dr. Kim: I think part of that was the fact that I always did want others to have this image that we had a great marriage. Part of it was pride, and part of it was that it was what I really wanted. I saw my parents always stay pretty private with their problems, and that influenced me.

Where is the trust in your marriage today? You have a lot of information about each other. Do you use it for good or not? Sometimes we use this information to get our way and don't even realize what we are doing. Sometimes our spouse is so used to it that they don't even notice it, but it is there. The wall is up and may have been up for a long time. If this is you, it's time to take that wall down! What you want in this second half of marriage is to be wall-less. The trust needs to flow like a river that never ends. That arsenal of information that you have acquired over the years about each other needs to be used solely for the good of each other and your marriage.

Questions for You:

- How do you use the information you have about each other?
- Do you use it to nurture, love, and come alongside each other, or to get your own way?
- What needs to stop?
- What needs to start?

2. Unforgiveness

Why do we often make the act of forgiveness so difficult? Why do we hesitate to do something that God actually tells us to do? When I teach singles and we are talking about what to look for in a future mate or even someone to date, I share this with them. If you are in a relationship where the person cannot forgive you, get out! Run and don't look back! You *will* screw up, so you have to be married to someone who will and can forgive you. If you are not, life will be really hard.

Most of us began marriage knowing we were marrying someone who could forgive our screwups. Yet for some, that becomes increasingly difficult over time. There are a myriad of reasons why we have trouble forgiving, but none of them justify unforgiveness. I can hear some of you now: "But you don't know what they did!" You are right, I don't, but I also know you will never have the marriage you want until these things are resolved, forgiven, and put far in the rearview mirror. For some it is a risk—maybe a big risk. You may be afraid that if you forgive, they will do it again. They may, but you will never have what you want until you take that risk. Why does God tell us to forgive? First, He knows there is no relationship without forgiveness. (See us and Jesus for an example.) Second, He is not asking us to do something that He has not done.

Nancy: In our marriage, there was never anything I thought was unforgivable. I've been really angry with you at times, but there wasn't anything I thought I couldn't forgive.

Dr. Kim: So how do you think we've handled forgiveness in our marriage?

Nancy: In our early marriage, we'd hold grudges. Even for probably the first 30 years of marriage, I was definitely bad about holding a grudge and giving the silent treatment. But I've just grown to find out that you don't deserve that.

Dr. Kim: Looking back, what was the point of the silent treatment?

Nancy: I wanted to punish you. Usually I'd hold out until you made the first move. I was pretty stubborn.

Dr. Kim: Early in our marriage, you would usually ask for forgiveness first. I don't think I did my part to apologize and to say I'm sorry, no matter who was wrong.

Nancy: It's still hard for me now to say that I'm sorry.

Dr. Kim: It sounds like you're saying that most of the unforgiveness was a manipulative thing.

Nancy: Yes. Absolutely.

Dr. Kim: Was there a time when you felt you needed to set those things aside? Talk a little bit about that.

Nancy: I think it was just a lot of life experience, and knowing how much you really love me. Growing into that trust and loving you back were big parts of that.

Dr. Kim: Say we were mentoring a couple before they got married, and you sensed after spending some time with the woman that she had trouble with forgiveness. How would you counsel her?

Nancy: I'd go back to her relationship with the Lord and how she accepted His forgiveness and what that means to her. I'd ask her about what Jesus did for her and what she deserved, and bring her back to her own human fallenness. I'd say to always remember that God says to forgive quickly and much. Am I really being faithful to Jesus if I don't forgive? And it's so much better when you do. It took me a while to get over grudge-holding, but it's such a sense of relief once you do forgive someone!

Dr. Kim: Can you think of any time when I said I forgave you but it felt like I didn't?

Nancy: No, you were always pretty honest.

Dr. Kim: Did you ever have any time when you said you forgave me but you were really holding on?

Nancy: No.

Dr. Kim: I think so too. I think we were pretty good about that. It wasn't like we always had a passionate reunion, but we'd ease back into it.

Questions for You:

- Is there something you have not forgiven your spouse for?
- If you answered yes, what steps do you need to take to heal this area of your life and your marriage? Maybe it is counseling. Maybe it is prayer. Whatever you need to do, please do it. Don't let unforgiveness ruin all you hoped and dreamed this second half of marriage would be for the two of you.

3. Someone or Something Else

The only "someones" who should be in your marriage are you, your spouse, and God! The only person or thing that needs to be second in your life (next to God) is your spouse. God is number one and your spouse is number two. It seems so simple on the written page. Then life gets in the way. You make an excuse. You spend a little more time away from home than you know is best. Your spouse is still on your list but pretty far from that number two position.

The real problem is that often those things we put ahead of our spouse are not bad things. It could be work, volunteering, hobbies, sports, friends, church, or fill in the blank. These are not bad things, but they become detrimental to your marriage when you elevate them above your spouse. The goal is for your spouse to always know he/she is number two day after day, month after month, and year after year. If you don't, you will gradually drift apart and the love you dreamed of sharing and growing in the second half will drift away too.

There are also things that take second place, or often even first place, that are just not okay. Things like drug abuse, alcohol abuse, pornography, or another person. It is so important for each of us to be honest about our vulnerabilities. We all have them. As much as I love and cherish Nancy, I have vulnerabilities. By being aware of them, I can pray for God to protect me and help me make decisions each day that honor Him and my marriage. The bottom line is this: Anyone or anything that is not good for your marriage needs to go, and you need to lock the door behind it. It is never worth the risk or worth giving in to the temptation. It's about drawing a hard line in the sand, then filling it with concrete so it becomes a boundary forever.

Dr. Kim: Nancy, what were some things that could take us away from putting God first and each other second?

Nancy: Obviously the kids. Then stuff you can buy. I just wanted the clothes and things like that, shopping for this and that for you and the kids. All the "stuff" of this world got in my way a lot. I also think that drinking was taking a huge part away from my relationship with God first, and also with you. It became too important to me.

Dr. Kim: Do you want to talk about that process of quitting?

Nancy: Yes. I felt like God had been telling me for a while. I think He first started pricking my conscience when we were adopting Grant, back in the early '70s, and we had to tell them at this particular home that we didn't drink. I felt so guilty that we were lying to them, but we did. I think God pricked me at that point. I thought maybe I shouldn't be drinking. I lived with that for years, and this is why I think I may be an alcoholic even though I wasn't knocked-down drunk or anything like that—I just wouldn't give it up. I didn't want to give it up. I enjoyed it too much. I looked forward to it too much. I'm not an expert, but I think that's a definition of alcoholism. I think that became so important to me that even though we didn't drink on weeknights, on Wednesday I would look forward to the weekend so we could drink. It became almost an obsession. I think any time you get that into something, it's not healthy.

Dr. Kim: So for you, at that point you were putting that above God.

Nancy: I was.

Dr. Kim: So talk about how you told me about that.

Nancy: It happened pretty suddenly, since God had been pricking my conscience for so long. One day, it was February 24, 2011, I was in the shower praying and thanking God. I thought, *Why don't I just quit drinking? Well, because I don't want to.* The Lord seemed to be speaking, not audibly, but to my heart, and said, "If you really want to put me first, this has got to get out of the way." So I made the commitment right then that I wasn't going to do that anymore. Of course, that night we were going to a wine tasting party. You asked me if I wanted a glass of wine, and I said that no, I had quit drinking.

Dr. Kim: I think my head spun. You hadn't told me, but you said you'd talked to God about it. We'd talked about it, but you had not talked as much to me.

Nancy: Well, if I talked about it, that would be an admission. If I talked about something God was telling me to do but I didn't do it, what would that say about me? Either I'm an alcoholic or just a bad Christian! It was easier to just ignore it.

Dr. Kim: I don't think there were too many things I put above you. I think there were things I pushed to accomplish. Like when we remodeled the house we bought and I was so adamant about putting in a swimming pool. You were adamant that we should not. Looking back, I see that I valued that more than your opinion and your wishes, and I pushed ahead with it.

In my own life, there are so many things we can get caught up in, and for a long time I didn't do a very good job evaluating how those would affect our marriage. I think I do a better job of that now and it's easier for me to take the time to look at that. I think that's something the Lord grew in me over time. Not that I can't fall into that still, but I have grown. It wasn't like I ever chased bad things, so if I compared myself to other people. I'd think, *I'm not having an affair. I'm not doing anything detrimental to my marriage*, so it seemed okay. But I could get caught up in buying things or making things happen.

Questions for You:

This is the time to get honest with yourself and with each other.

- Is there something or someone in your life that needs to go?
- What or who is it?
- What is your first step in letting go?
- Is there a "good thing" in your life that is not good for your marriage?
- What is it?
- What is your action step?
- Do you need to eliminate it altogether or simply put it in its proper priority spot in your life?

Moving On

Let's go back to that question I asked a few pages ago: How would you rate your love in your marriage today on a 1 to 10 scale, with 10 being amazing? There are no wrong answers. Sure, you may wish your number was higher than it is, but we have to have a starting place. Look at it this way: if you are not honest with your answer here, you are defeating the purpose of reading this book.

Over the years of our marriage, I think we have hit every number at some point. We had our ones and twos. Most of them were in the early years of our marriage, but they still reared their heads at times. We learned to address the issues and resolve them before we got stuck there. If you are a one or a two—or even a zero—there is hope. You can really only go in one direction, and that is up. Three is the first step up for a number of people and a sign that things are slipping for others. I think fours, fives, sixes, and sevens can be the most difficult. Their marriage is not where they would like it to be but it's not bad enough to do anything about it. These couples can get complacent. They can become the couch potatoes of marriage. They are in the game but they are not moving.

Then there are eights and nines, and believe it or not, that can be a problem for some. Sure there is celebration when we hit these numbers, but some couples or individuals will take it that they won and the race is over. Do you know what that will do for your marriage? It will take you back to a five or lower. Staying at an eight or a nine year after year takes effort. It takes a lot of effort. It takes a lot of forgiveness, empathy, and compromise. It's truly putting God first and your spouse second every day. It's being a servant, as Jesus modeled so well for us. Guess what happens when you do those things? Your marriage keeps getting better. The better it gets, the better you forgive, compromise, show empathy, and serve. Can you even imagine what this marriage would be like? I can. We have been there. Don't get me wrong, we are not there every day, but it is our goal every day. We have tasted the fruit and it is sweet. We are motivated to fight to stay there. No one and nothing can rob us of this.

I left out ten but I left it out on purpose. For us ten is the ultimate and ten really does make us think we have arrived. So for Nancy and me, although we will strive for a ten, we will never say we are there. That keeps us on track. It keeps us looking for new ways to grow. It makes each new day something to look forward to. Today as I am writing I would give us an eight. On the day you read this, if you want to know where we are that day, email me (drkim@awesomemarriage.com) and I will tell you!

Dr. Kim: Nancy, on that scale, how would you have rated our marriage over the years?

Nancy: I think when we were first married, it was a 1½! I was just unhappy moving away from my family. I left all my sorority friends and college friends and went to a new school. In the sixth year, when I thought we were supposed to get a divorce, that was really bad. It wasn't anything you had done; it was just me being basically an unhappy person.

Dr. Kim: Do you feel like at the time you blamed me for that?

Nancy: I think I blamed you passive-aggressively for living here when I just wanted to be back with my family and friends. It would make me crazy that you'd act like this is such a great city. I agree with you now, but back then it was like, "What is he talking about?" It would make me angry. I was immature. I think our story is unique, in that for most couples, when they're newlyweds, the wife is just starry-eyed in love, and if not, they often end up divorced.

Dr. Kim: One thing that's good about us is that we were so immature and so young but we did make it. I think God had a lot to do with that. There were a lot of rough things.

Nancy: A lot of life is just gutting it out and committing that we were going to make it through the hard times. We used the good times as a booster. And I would say we're a 9½ right now. I feel so secure in our love for each other—the selfless kind of love. Just to the point that if something happened to you I don't think there's any way I could remarry. Before, I thought I might, but now I just can't see that. That's how deep it is.

Dr. Kim: I think so. Since we're talking about this stage of marriage, the goal is to get to where you're that comfortable. I always want to make sure people know that we haven't always been here. I think sometimes people who have just met us could look at us and think, *Their whole marriage has been that way,* but it hasn't.

Nancy: No. And we have a lot of friends who are where we are. Yet there are those out there who are married 50, 60, 70 years and can't stand each other. I think that's so sad!

Dr. Kim: So if a couple came to us and said they just celebrated their fiftieth anniversary, like we did, and they didn't have what we have and wanted to know our secret, what would you tell them?

Nancy: At that point, I think they need to go back, look at all the things in their marriage, and see if there's any good there that they can salvage. I do think professional help is so good when you're miserable in your marriage. You just need to get some help and be guided out of that. God can do it, but you both have to really be in prayer and seeking it.

Dr. Kim: And people need to know that it's never too late. If people want it, they can still get there.

Nancy: I don't think God was there witnessing your marriage and expecting that you'd live life miserably. He doesn't want divorce. He wants you to look to Him and His principles and His love for yourself and for your mate.

Dr. Kim: Right. And I think it's some of the things we've talked about as individuals and as a couple. But if you've been married a long time, don't give up on having that.

Nancy: That's right. Too many people have, which is sad.

Dr. Kim: I remember when we were a lot younger and we'd go out to dinner and see an older couple, and you could just tell whether they were connected or not. I remember one couple we looked at and they were holding hands under the table. They were probably in their 80s. You can tell. And if somebody wants that, I think you can have it.

Questions for You:

- Define what being a servant means in your marriage.
- When is it difficult for you to be a servant to your spouse and when does it come easier?
- How will you serve each other today?

Growing Your Love

Remember that "love" as a noun is a feeling and "love" as a verb is an action. The feeling part of love is interesting. When it is there, I cannot get enough of Nancy. I can literally follow her around like a puppy dog. Every look, word, or touch makes my heart race. Then there are days when I feel close to nothing. Maybe we disagreed on something or she said yes to an invitation for us without asking me first and I do not want to go. The puppy dog walks away.

If I based my love for Nancy on feelings, I would be riding the roller coaster of marriage day in and day out. That would be nauseating—literally! So on those days when the love feels high, I embrace them with everything that I have. On the days when the love feeling is low, I remember the commitment I have in marriage and that the "love feeling high" days will return.

Do our feelings motivate our actions or do our actions produce our feelings? What do you think? Is this a "which comes first" thing, like the chicken and the egg, where you can make a decent argument both ways? Let's break this down. If I am feeling love toward Nancy, it is likely that my actions will reflect that feeling. If I am acting in ways that show my love and Nancy receives my actions and returns the love to me, my love feelings will most likely manifest themselves.

Here's the problem. In scenario one, where I let my feelings lead to actions, what if my feelings of love never come? Does that mean my actions of love are never triggered? In scenario two, where actions produce feelings, what if my actions never trigger the love feelings in Nancy and she never responds with the acts of love that I hope for? What if I am left with nothing?

Now that I have you totally confused, let me make a confession: that is just what I was trying to do. Deciding which comes first in these scenarios is dependent on one thing: feelings. If I feel the love, I act. If I act and get loving feelings in return, I feel loved. In other words, if the love feeling does not come, I fail because ultimately I wanted the love feeling. If we spend our marriage waiting for our loving feelings to start before we show our love, then our marriage will suffer. In this pattern, love is conditional—we give love only when we feel loving, when we feel loved, or when our spouse makes us happy. With this cycle we are very likely to get stuck in patterns of misunderstanding, miscommunication, hurt feelings, or scorekeeping. It's the marriage roller coaster again.

Don't worry. I'm not going to leave you high and dry. Here's the answer: obedience. What does obedience have to do with love? Now you are asking the right question.

Let me give you an example. Most people would agree that Jesus is the ultimate authority of love. He loved everyone. He died for those He loved. As He hung on that cross, He was there because of the feeling of love that led Him to pray compassionately for His accusers, "Father, forgive them." He was there because of the obedient action of love. He did not have to go to the cross. He could have spoken and called angels to the rescue, but He didn't. His love for us, me and you, drove Him to the cross. Why? Behind the love was obedience. He was doing what He knew He would do from the beginning of time. Did He hesitate? Well, He did ask His Father to let the cup pass from Him. In other words, "Do I still have to do this?" The answer was yes, and Jesus set His eyes on the cross. Obedience ignited by love.

I love Nancy. Every day I pray to be the husband God created me to be for her. Every day there are times I don't especially want to put out the effort to be that husband. There are days I don't. Yet every day when I pray that prayer, I know God will equip me for the role. Here is the kicker. Deep in my heart I know that if I want to be that husband, I have to be obedient to God. It doesn't matter what Nancy does or does not do. It doesn't matter if she is gushing over me with love or is very distant. It does not matter if she does not do even one loving action for me. My role is, with God's help, to be the husband God wants me to be each day. My job is to be obedient to God.

As I have traveled this road of obedience, God has taught me a lot. First, He has never asked me to do anything that is not good for me, Nancy, or our marriage. That alone is huge! Second, at the end of the day, I have the opportunity to say to God that with His help, I did a pretty good job as a husband today because I was obedient to Him. Does this happen every day? No. Do I try almost every day? Yes. Obedience.

This is the amazing part: When I am obedient to God and His role for me as a husband to Nancy, it stokes two fires. One is "feeling love" for both Nancy and for God. Two is the "action love" that plays out as I show her my love through my actions, directed by God. This is a win/win. It's the walk-off field goal as the game clock hits zero!

Dr. Kim: What are some ways you've been obedient to God in our marriage?

Nancy: I think by swallowing my pride to say, "I'm sorry." It was hard to pry my fingers off the pride of winning an argument or be the first to say sorry.

Dr. Kim: What got you to the point of knowing God wanted you to do that?

Nancy: I think it was growing in a relationship with God, realizing how much He loves me in spite of everything, and realizing how much you love me, which I think is the most a human being on earth could. It makes a huge difference when you start realizing how loved you are.

Dr. Kim: I think that's a good point. I think some people really have a hard time accepting that. Maybe you did for a while.

Nancy: I did. I had a hard time with that. It all starts with your relationship with God.

Dr. Kim: I can think of times I was upset with you. Now we recover pretty quickly, but we could push each other's buttons pretty well. I would think of ways I could punish you or make it hard for you, and I could feel God saying, "What are you doing? That's not what I want you to do. You're supposed to forgive. You're supposed to lead this family and be an example." Most of the time I heard that.

As I got older I experienced more of His love, and your love, and for me that was a lot. I didn't really feel confident in your love for me earlier in our marriage. A lot of insecure behaviors grew out of that. I guess I was trying to keep you. I think as I saw more of your love it was easier for me to let go of that.

Nancy: When did that happen for you?

Dr. Kim: Probably when I went into ministry in 1983. Going to seminary completely changed and deepened my faith. I thought I was a good Christian before, but there wasn't much depth to it.

Nancy: Your relationship with God grows if you let it. Just like a marriage, with God's help it will grow if you let it grow.

Questions for You:

- Do you trust God to let Him guide your actions toward your spouse?
- If not, what stands between you and Him?
- What would obedience to God as a spouse look like in your marriage?

8 Ways to Keep Growing the Love

1. Toss the "Divorce" Card

I think that this is a given, but I still see couples or individuals who hold this over their marriage like it was the ace of spades. The "divorce" card. If the option of divorce is not taken off the table and thrown away, you will never know the fullness of love in your marriage. You cannot be all in if you're considering getting out. A healthy marriage is one where both people can be totally and completely transparent and vulnerable with each other. That only happens when both feel secure and safe in their marriage. That will never happen in a marriage with the threat of divorce still in play.

Questions for You:

- Have you taken the option of divorce off the table?
- If not, would you do that today?
- What does it mean to both of you to have divorce no longer be an option in your marriage?

Dr. Kim: When do you think we did this in our marriage?

Nancy: We let that go way too long. At least, I think I did.

Dr. Kim: I think after you resolved to stay married in our sixth year, I think that really did take it off the table.

Nancy: I think you're right.

Dr. Kim: I think there were still things in our arsenal we used.

Nancy: Well, I knew it would make you maddest if I said anything about divorce.

Dr. Kim: You're right. I don't think your intent was there, but you could use it to manipulate.

Nancy: Exactly. I was just trying to hurt you.

Dr. Kim: Talk about that.

Nancy: Well, I knew that when we were in the heat of an argument, that would just settle it right there. It didn't.

Dr. Kim: No. It didn't.

2. Marriage Goals

As a couple, what are you doing right now to intentionally grow your love for each other? Whatever you are doing that is working, keep doing it. Then try this idea: set some goals together for your marriage. Start with a list of the things that are important to you in your marriage today. Then add to your list anything that you would like to have in your marriage that is not there today.

Next, separate the items on your list into three groups: daily, short term, and long term. Daily items are the things you can do each day to show love, help each other out, and enrich each other's lives. Short-term items are the things you would like to build into your marriage over the next year. And long-term items are the things that you want to build into your marriage over the next five to ten years. Now you have a road map to take with you as you drive down the marriage highway. Discuss what each of you will specifically do to build all these goals into your marriage. Encourage each other in what you are doing. Every six months, look at your lists and see how you are doing. You can always change or update your lists.

Questions for You:

- What are your daily goals for your marriage?
- What are your short-term goals for your marriage?
- What are your long-term goals for your marriage?

Nancy: Daily, we continue praying together. We make sure we don't go to bed angry. Daily we say, "I love you," and mean it. Daily we aim to have a servant's heart for each other.

Dr. Kim: I think what you helped build into our marriage was communication time every day. Making sure we sat down to talk and touch base. If there's something we need to talk about, we have that space and we do it.

Nancy: Then shorter term, we continue growing individually as well as with the Lord. I love being part of a Bible study. I'm the kind of person who needs something structured like that to keep me on track. We do our devotional every evening, but I just need that time by myself to help me grow.

Dr. Kim: I think that's really a good point. These don't have to be things you always do together. The things we do that are good for us turn out to be good for our marriage as well.

Nancy: All of us have a personal relationship with God. Then if you're married, you become one and have a relationship with God together; but if you let your personal one-on-one time with God go, you're just hobbling along.

Dr. Kim: I agree. I'm really consistent with my morning quiet time and that's been huge. There are times when I don't even remember what I've prayed about or what I've read, but I've been consistent, and God has really used that. That helps me focus. If I get up and I'm rushed and don't have time for that quiet time,

I kind of feel naked the whole day. Like I don't have that connection.

I think another short-term thing is continuing to work on our sex life. We'll talk more about sex in another part of the book, but that's one thing we focus on keeping healthy. We probably know people who have kind of let that slide as they've gotten a little older.

Nancy: They think that because they're older they shouldn't do it anymore. Maybe it takes more effort, or your knee hurts or something, but that's such a big part.

Dr. Kim: I think so. Of course, early in marriage the physical aspect is certainly a big part. We enjoyed that a lot together. But as we've grown, it has deepened to where it consumes us emotionally, physically, even spiritually,

Nancy: I do hope that people start experiencing that at a much earlier age than we did. And you may have to make some adjustments, but it's worth it to keep that alive.

Dr. Kim: So, long term, what are we doing to keep our marriage where it is?

Nancy: Serving together, evangelizing, and trying to see how many people we can bring before Jesus. And I would like to see us spend more effort and resources for the good of others. I think I was too tight-fisted for most of my life, but now I want to make up for that with generosity.

Dr. Kim: I think that when either one of us had something we wanted to give to, we just accepted that and the other person would come on board with it.

Nancy: Yeah. But when I look back on it, I think that we could have done so much better. We didn't really understand until about 15 years ago that there's the tithe, then there's the offering. I can remember having what we'd call a "God account" we contributed to. Instead of 10 percent being just for our local church, we included everything in that, all of our giving, like when we'd make a contribution to someone. It's been so much more exciting now that we give 10 percent to the church, plus the offering—totally separate things that we do. I'd like to see us be more openhanded.

Dr. Kim: I think God has shown us the joy in letting go and being generous.

Nancy: It really is more blessed to give than to receive. I just wasn't trusting God very much. I came from a family that didn't have too much. I was never in need, but we had to watch pennies, and I brought that into marriage. A lot of times I could call that being a "good steward," but really I was just holding on to things for me, you, and our kids. But it needed to be more openhanded for whoever God brought into our path.

Dr. Kim: We were doing the tithe, and that was kind of checking off the box. But the joy in it is what God is showing us. We were always obedient to that, but we didn't really let God show us what generosity was all about.

3. Dealing with Disappointments

Each of you stop and take a minute to answer this question: Is there anything in your marriage that makes you sad?

I surveyed a group of couples and these are some of their answers:

- "Taking each other for granted"
- "When my husband's family hurts him"

- "The thought of losing my spouse"
- "Not listening to each other"

How did you answer the question? In every marriage there are some sad things. Most of us do not like to deal with sad or disappointing things. We may stuff them down or cover them up like they do not exist. We may feel helpless and hopeless, but I do not believe that is where God wants us to be.

Here is my suggestion. When sad things happen, you can come together and actually grow your love for each other during this time. It doesn't matter if just one of you is sad or if both of you are sad; the way you handle these times will make a difference one way or the other.

Let's talk about how these times can grow your love. First, decide if you have any control over the situation. Sometimes we can do something to make a difference and other times we cannot. My advice is that if there is something you can do about a situation, do it. Support each other and stand together. On the other hand, if the situation is out of your control, you have to accept that fact.

It is not always easy, but here is the reality. You can keep spending time and effort on something that you cannot change, or you can say, "There is nothing I can do about this," and let it go. Now God has you where He wants you, and that is turning to Him. Turning to God actually gives you something that you can do together! You can pray. You can seek God's wisdom and intervention. God will hear your prayers and He will show up. It is in those times when we think we have nothing left that we realize we have everything. This is the Creator of the universe. He has this!

Questions for You:

- What makes you sad in your marriage today?
- What can you do about it together?

Nancy: I think now that I'm older, one thing that makes me sad is when I think about our health. It's going to give out sometime. I think about how I want Jesus to come back, yet I want to be married to you, and I won't be married to you anymore in heaven. It's kind of a lot to take stock of in these last 10, 15, 20 years, or whatever God gives us. We don't have the rest of our lives with a great span in front of us anymore. So I want to use that time wisely, but it can make me sad to really start thinking about that.

Dr. Kim: Does that make you want to be more intentional about using the time that we do have?

Nancy: Yes, absolutely.

Dr. Kim: I think it does too. I've told you recently how much I look forward to coming home to you each day. Sometimes I'll think about it in the middle of the day and look at my watch to check how long it will be until I see you. Almost like when we were dating and I couldn't wait to pick you up on campus to take you to class. I think it's because we really have worked at nurturing that. During our marriage, one thing that has made me sad at times is when someone hurt you.

Nancy: Any time someone hurts a person you love, you want to defend them. Initially you'll be angry toward that other person. Then I think that you have to let the Lord take over there and teach you what He wants to teach you.

Dr. Kim: If I let myself, I can get sad that we have fewer years left together than we used to. But I don't really let myself stay there. I think if you stay in that sadness, it can really put a damper on where you are right now, and I want to enjoy where we are in this stage of life and live it to the fullest.

Nancy: It's a shame we didn't do that all along. You just think you'll live forever.

Dr. Kim: You do. But we were learning all along. Looking back I think we did a pretty good job all along. We always had fun together, and we've always communicated well.

Nancy: We've always been best friends. And that's helped us through it all.

4. Appreciate the Good Things

Let's get out of the dumps by answering our next question. What makes you happy in your marriage? Again I polled a group and here are a few of their answers:

- "My husband's cooking"
- "When we are being considerate of each other"
- "Knowing that my husband is a godly man"
- "Holding hands"
- "Finding ways to please my wife"
- "I love how we communicate, even if we do not agree"
- "I love our commitment to our marriage"
- "Snuggling up to each other"

As I look at these answers, all of them are "love growers." It is also interesting that the things that made these people the happiest in their marriages were the simple things. Contentment in marriage is not about money or power. It is not about possessions or elaborate vacations. It is about those things that connect a husband and wife, and that connection grows love.

I have said for a long time that marriage is not rocket science. We don't need to understand something as complicated as the science that goes into propelling a rocket into space in order to explain what sends a marriage soaring. What fuels a marriage are the daily, simple, purposeful things that we do for and with our spouses. They make a difference and they will grow your love.

> **Questions for You:**
> - What makes you happy in your marriage today?
> - What are your "love growers"?

Dr. Kim: So, Nancy, what about things that make you happy in marriage? What are some things that have grown our marriage?

Nancy: I think, like you said, spending time together. I look forward to you coming home in the evening and our evenings together. We enjoy most of the same things, and I like doing those things with you. Communication.

Dr. Kim: I think something we've done in our whole marriage, and have picked back up recently, is exploring together. Get in the car when we've got some time and drive somewhere or explore a neighborhood we've never been to before. I think keeping some adventure is good for our marriage. We started hiking in COVID, since there wasn't much else to do! But we've enjoyed it and I think we'll keep it up. It's different than if I just started hiking by myself. It wouldn't have been as much fun. Plus I really like you walking in front of me because then I can watch you.

Nancy: *(Laughs)*

5. Be a Good Student

Being a student of your spouse is a marriage-long project. I believe that a lifetime is not long enough to learn everything about your spouse. We grow and we change, and if we are not intentional about studying our spouse, we may look at them one day and wonder, "Who are you?" Okay, that's a little extreme, but being a student of your spouse means that you are tuned in to them every day. It is not something we do without effort, but the rewards are wonderful.

Nancy is my best friend. She has been since we were dating in college. She still has those qualities I fell in love with but now I have even more to love. If I had not intentionally studied her, I would have missed out on so much. But I didn't always do this well. I took a few "semesters" off and then later had to play catchup.

Being a student of your spouse is not complicated; it is just being intentional. Do you know your spouse's love language? Nancy's is quality time. So in our marriage, I am going to learn the most about Nancy when I fulfill her love language. It shows her I care and that she is important to me and that I love her. When she feels loved by me, she shares her life with me. She shares funny things and serious things. She shares fears, cares, concerns, doubts, joys, and so much more. She becomes the teacher of a subject she is the expert on: herself. Me? I am the student.

Questions for You:

- When it comes to being a student of your spouse, how good a student are you?
- How could you be a better student?
- Share something with each other that you recently learned about each other.

Nancy: Now we can almost finish each other's sentences. Like when you call and say, "You know what I was thinking would be good for dinner?" and it's usually the same thing I was thinking of.

Dr. Kim: It's so weird how that happens. It's happened a lot.

Nancy: Scary.

Dr. Kim: Or cool! How do you feel like you fulfilled my love language? How has knowing that my love language is words of affirmation helped you show that for me?

Nancy: I look for ways I can encourage you, tell you what a good job you're doing. I definitely didn't do enough of that early on. I'm kind of trying to make up for lost time.

Dr. Kim: I think you always have, but you have definitely gotten better at it.

Nancy: As I've grown in my love for you, I notice things more. It's not so much about me.

Dr. Kim: I think knowing that your love language is quality time really helps, because I can be selfish with my time. But I know and can see the difference when we spend quality time. I used to kind of think that if I spent quality time with you one weekend you wouldn't need it the next, but that didn't work. Your tank got empty and it needed to be filled again.

Nancy: True.

6. Accept Differences

Have you noticed ways that you and your spouse are different? Not just physically, but in so many ways. It may be your likes and dislikes. It may be the way you look at a particular situation. It may be how you load the dishwasher! Most couples fight over their differences at least to some extent. It's the second half of marriage and you are trying to love each other better. Put the gloves down.

Here is a novel idea. Why not accept each other's differences? Why not see each other's differences as opportunities to grow and to learn? You probably know by now that differences will either pull the two of you apart or bond you closer together. If you let them pull you apart, a portion of that love you are trying to build will go too. I believe that God made us all unique and that our differences are what make our marriages truly special. If Nancy and I were exactly alike, I think we would have bored each other to death a long time ago. I get enough of me as it is! Our differences have been frustrating at times but without them neither of us would be who we are today. God used Nancy's differences to grow me, to teach me, and to help mold me more into who He created me to be. He did the same for her.

Questions for You:

- What are the differences in your spouse that bother you?
- What if you prayed for God to mold your spouse into who God wants them to be?
- What if you both prayed that prayer?
- What if you began looking at the differences as opportunities instead of obstacles? Can you imagine the difference it would make?
- If you want a way to boost your love for each other up a point or two, embrace each other's differences. Think of one way you can do that.

Dr. Kim: So what differences do we have from each other that we had to accept? Are there any we still struggle with?

Nancy: Well, for one, there's the way you drive. I have not come to terms with that. You take your time, but when I get in the car I get impatient and I just want to be there already!

Dr. Kim: Well, it's not like I just started that; it's been that way since you met me. I think we've accepted a lot of our differences. I think over time we've lined up a lot. Our beliefs and values are very much in line. Politically we line up together. We don't argue about much. We discuss things, but we don't argue. Our differences mainly were figuring out how to have a life and a marriage that were different from your family and unique to us. I always thought my family was healthier than yours.

Nancy: Well, they were.

Dr. Kim: Yes, but we didn't need to try to be them. For a while I thought our marriage should fit their template, and that held us back.

Nancy: But they gave us a pattern to go by.

Dr. Kim: We saw unconditional love, patience, and respect…

Nancy: …and commitment, and overlooking each other's flaws.

Dr. Kim: We have become a lot like them in those ways. Are there any other differences?

Nancy: Well, we haven't lost our uniqueness. You're still you, you know. I'm still go-go-go, while you're more laid back. They're not bad, just different.

7. Moving on from Mistakes

Have you ever made a mistake in your marriage? If you answered no, email me. My email address is a few pages back. We all make mistakes in marriage. I counsel so many people that are stuck in their past mistakes. Their spouse has forgiven them. God has forgiven them. Yet they cannot forgive themselves. When that happens, your love in your marriage will not grow. Not even a little bit. Why? Because you think that you are unworthy of love.

Here is the thing: you are worthy of love. I know. I used to do the same thing to myself. I would make a mistake. I would tell God and Nancy that I was sorry. I knew they both forgave me but I thought it came too easy. It's an interesting phenomenon how we think we have to suffer to be forgiven.

From a 30,000-foot view, the idea of not forgiving myself makes no sense, but too often on the ground it somehow seems to be true. It is not! So you may wonder how I broke out of that pattern. It was not easy, but some real truths began to replace the lies I was believing, like "I am not worthy of love." First, if God forgives me, why do I think that I have the right to not forgive myself? He created everything. He knows me better than I know myself. He knows the thoughts I think that no one else knows. All of that and I am forgiven. Jesus died to redeem all my sins and mistakes, and all of yours. Not accepting His forgiveness is like telling Jesus His sacrifice was not enough. I never want to let that be the case! I want to willingly agree that there is no better or greater sacrifice, and no one more worthy than Him. I want to accept His forgiveness, knowing that this is what frees me up to live and love well.

Second, if I learn from my mistakes, God has a way of redeeming them. I have a temper. It does not come out very often today but there was a time I wore it right below the surface. I embarrassed myself and Nancy way too many times. It was becoming a wedge between us. I would always apologize to her but I never took seriously making any changes, and so the cycle repeated. Through some really serious talks with Nancy, I knew I had to change. I was repeating my mistake instead of learning from it.

Today, I still feel the anger at times but I have learned to harness it. God opened my eyes and let me see the damage I was doing. I embarrassed Nancy. I lashed out at people I didn't even know and it was not doing a lot for my witness as a Christian. God took this mistake and used it as another step to grow me into who He designed me to be. Let me tell you how good God is. When I talk about my temper in the past, people look at me like I am nuts. They can't believe it. I am a different person. Through all of this I not only experienced more of God's love, but I also experienced more of Nancy's love.

Questions for You:

- You will make mistakes. How will you handle the mistakes you make? How are you doing at forgiving yourself?
- Is there anything you have not forgiven yourself for?
- If there is, take it before God. He has the answer you need. Free yourself up to grow the love between you, your spouse, and God.

Nancy: Sometimes I look back and I catch myself rueing certain things that I said or did. But I'm really working on that because I've sought the Lord's forgiveness on that and on things I've specifically asked your forgiveness for. I need to forgive myself for those mistakes and shortcomings. If it wasn't for me, we would have had a better marriage a lot sooner.

Dr. Kim: But I wouldn't have had any marriage at all if you weren't in it!

Nancy: I'm just saying, this is where healthy families can push a healthy person out of the nest. You helped me become healthy. I'm passionate about this, because healthier parents can raise kids that are healthy and can go out in the world as healthy, responsible citizens, parents, providers, and homemakers, whatever they're called to. A healthy marriage can do so much good for this world. It can make such an impact, and it's what we need in this world.

Dr. Kim: So do you feel like you've forgiven yourself for most things now?

Nancy: I have to catch myself sometimes, but I do feel like I have.

Dr. Kim: I think so. Forgiveness has always been pretty easy for me. That may be because of the way I grew up. My parents never held anything I did over me. I was disciplined and then it was never brought up again. I think that taught me about forgiveness, that you do forgive and then you move on. The only things I have struggled with, I think of times when I felt like I hurt you. Those were hard because I never wanted to hurt you. If I hurt you emotionally, that was hard for me.

Nancy: I can't think of anything like that.

Dr. Kim: Most of them were probably earlier on. Someone told me a long time ago that if God can forgive you, why can't you forgive yourself? That was probably the best counsel I heard about that.

Nancy: That's right. I heard someone say that to dwell on things and not forgive yourself is like thinking Jesus should get back onto the cross and be re-nailed. That's powerful. In not forgiving yourself, it's like you're saying that His death, burial, and resurrection weren't enough.

8. Generosity

The word "generosity" is used a lot today. It is the quality of being kind and generous. I like that definition. I think generosity can be a lifestyle and an awesome thing for a marriage. If we were to put the template of generosity over a marriage, what would we see? This is where the word "kind" jumps out at me. It's kindness in the way we speak to our spouse, in our actions toward our spouse, and in our behaviors with our spouse. It's looking at our spouse as a gift from God and thanking God every day for that gift by being kind.

Then let's look at "generous." We can be generous in the quality time we give our spouse. It is taking the opportunities that are right in front of us every day and not letting them pass by. It's delighting in your spouse and looking for ways to surprise them to keep your marriage exciting. It is doing all of these with joy. That's the difference.

It's the same with the principle of generosity with our finances. When we give, is it because we feel we have to? Is it an obligation? Do we give with a little bit of resentment? If so, it is still giving but it is not generosity. It becomes generosity when we give because we want to. It is never out of obligation and there is never resentment attached to it. The same is true of showing generosity to our spouse. If it is a "have to" or an obligation, it is not generosity. If it is because we want to and are always looking for ways to be kind and generous to our spouse, that is true generosity and both of you reap the benefits.

Questions for You:

- How do you show generosity to each other?
- What are some ways you can be kind to each other?
- What does being generous to each other look like in your marriage?

Nancy: For me it's listening. Time. Serving. Trying to figure out what I can do for you to make your life better on a given day.

Dr. Kim: For me it's the actions. It's also the attitude of being kind toward you, taking the time to hear you, and doing things that make you feel valued. I think that's part of being generous toward you. I think when I do things out of obligation, it's different than being generous. Generosity just flows out of my heart.

Nancy: Absolutely. Generosity is not "having to"; it's wanting to.

Of these eight ways to grow your marriage, how would you rank them as far as importance to you in your marriage? Is there one or more that is an obstacle for the two of you? If we put the eight into categories, only one is in the "check it off and move on" category: taking divorce off the table. Intentional growth, being a student of your spouse, accepting differences, and generosity are lifestyle points. These are the ones that you repeat daily. It's like four pills your doctor says you have to take every day if you want to stay alive. These four are not only to keep your marriage alive but also to help it to grow and thrive each day.

The things that make you sad are your red flags in your marriage. They let you know that there is something the two of you need to work on together. The things that make you happy are things to celebrate and they are also great motivators to keep working on and growing your marriage. Seven of the ways to grow that we looked at are between you, your spouse, and God. He is our source of strength, wisdom, and power as we grow. Finally, moving on from mistakes and forgiving ourselves is between God and each individual spouse. Sure, the other spouse can pray and be supportive, but when it comes to conditions of the heart, we need to let God do His work in us. He is the heart changer!

Love Is...

Love is a lot of things. We can use the word "love" to describe our affection for anything from Taco Bell to our favorite sport, favorite entertainer, favorite color, and on and on. If someone just learning English tried to figure out what the word "love" means in our culture, I think they would be very confused. Let's focus on love in the second half of marriage and four things love is.

1. Love Is Leading

The Bible does not say a husband is to be the leader in the first half of marriage and then he gets to retire from that role. I don't see a way out of this. We don't get to quit on leading. Jesus is pretty clear when He says, "Whoever wants to be great must become a servant. Whoever wants to be first among you must be your slave. That is what the Son of Man has done: He came to serve, not be served—and then to give away his life in exchange for the many who are held hostage" (Matthew 20:26-28, The Message).

It still goes back to serving our spouse and being completely unselfish. What does it look like to lead in the second half of your marriage? The bullet list of what a wife needs from her husband today as a leader is not much different from what she needed on day one of marriage. Here is my take on what a wife needs:

- A sense of safety and security
- To know her husband will protect her, watch over her, and keep her from harm
- To know her husband would never knowingly hurt her

I don't pretend that I have always done these well. It has been a series of trials and errors. I had to know what each of those meant to Nancy. What made her feel safe and secure? How could I best protect her and what did she need protection from? Was I doing anything that was hurting her? That was a tough one for me. Some of the things that hurt her were not on my radar. When that happened, my standard response was, "That shouldn't hurt you." If I did not intend harm, how could she take it as harmful? I had to grow into accepting that if it hurt her, it hurt her no matter my intent and it had to stop!

I have never met a man who said, "I have leadership in marriage down and I have from the beginning." (Again, if you have, email me. We will write a book together!) So if you are thinking, *I have blown this so many times in the first half; how can I do better in the second half?* then here are four steps to get you on the right track:

1. Set a level playing field. If you have ever hurt your wife in any way, tell her you are sorry and that from today on you will never knowingly hurt her again.
2. Ask her what you can do to help her feel protected and cared for. Then do it.
3. Ask her about her fears and then together lay those at the feet of God in prayer.
4. Pray and ask God to show you daily how to be a courageous and selfless leader in your marriage.

Honestly, I think we make leading a lot more difficult than it is. If I get all the junk, like pride and selfishness, out of the way, then serving my wife is pretty easy.

Questions for You:

- As a husband, what are your leadership struggles in your marriage?
- What stands in the way of you being the leader God created you to be?
- Which of the four steps to get on track will you begin doing?

Dr. Kim: Early in marriage, I didn't understand what leadership was. I thought it was pretty much me being in control. I think it came off as me being controlling and trying to kind of tell you what to do. I think because of your personality type, you rebelled against that.

Nancy: Yes, that's definitely true. I definitely rebelled. I think there's a lot of rebellion that goes on today. I don't think that a lot of people understand the biblical definition of leading together in a marriage.

Dr. Kim: So when do you think I figured out how to lead the way God wanted me to?

Nancy: I think it was when you deepened your faith and began to get more deeply into your ministry.

Dr. Kim: I think so. I think in the culture I grew up with, men were the dominant ones, and I think that wasn't right. We had to learn to lead in the ways God wanted us to lead.

Nancy: I agree. You and I are prime examples of the end of that era, basically. Where the man was the "say-so" in the family and the wife was basically subservient. Today, women rebel against that, and I don't blame them because I think there are a lot of dominating tendencies from a man if he takes that perspective.

I think we need to talk more about what it means to lead together. I know God intends you to be head of the home, just as Christ is the head of the Church, but that doesn't mean the wife is less significant. She is also the head in her role as wife and mother, and she is also a leader in the family. I think we were created with the husband to be stronger physically and in a role of protection. The mother also protects her kids, but the husband is basically the warrior for his family.

Dr. Kim: I think some rebellion against this idea comes from how men have gone about leadership. If you take the idea of leadership and look at Jesus' example, that is how we were meant to lead—as a servant leader. And He died for us. I think guys think they can lead in their work or business the same way they do in the home, and that doesn't work. At work, if we have people who work under us, we tell them what to do and they do it. That's not the way marriage is supposed to be. I almost wish we had a different word to use that would fit our culture more so that people could understand it. I do think it's important to understand what God's plan is, and there is a lot of responsibility placed on the husband. He is to serve, protect, and die to himself for the sake of the family, which is really hard to do in a culture that tells you it's all about you.

Nancy: I agree with that. I like to think of myself as serving with you, at your side, rather than under you. Yet I defer to you when it needs physical strength or help with a final decision if it's within your area of expertise.

Dr. Kim: I look at it as a symbiotic relationship. We're side by side, we're equals, yet we both have gifts that the other doesn't have, so we're indispensable to each other. We're there together. I do think that God puts it on us to lead in the way He wants us to lead.

Nancy: Exactly.

Dr. Kim: I think my wins as a leader have been when I got that. When I listen to you, like if we have a decision to make, I value what you tell me, then we talk about it. Then I think that when we come together, we're usually able to be on the same page together and come to the same decision.

2. Love Is Following

I guess if leading is a little countercultural, following is a lot countercultural. Why would a wife want to follow her husband? Even if she wants to follow his leadership, it seems to be very difficult for many women to do. Right now, I am wondering why I even included leading and following in this book on the second half of marriage. If a couple got the concept in the first half of marriage, they will see the value and most likely keep it up. If a couple never embraced this concept in the first half of marriage, will they even consider it now? Actually, I know exactly why I am including it, so bear with me.

The Bible makes it clear that it is part of God's plan for marriage. Let's unpack this and see if we can understand the why behind the plan. God made man and woman. God created marriage. Men and women are different by design. Each has specific roles in a marriage. Each role is indispensable to the life and wellbeing of the marriage. The leading and following defined in the Bible are for marriage, not for work or the outside world. It is part of God's plan to give us awesome marriages.

I believe that wives have trouble following their husbands' lead because their husbands do not lead. At least not in the way God intended. For Nancy and me, this was a big learning experience. I knew I was supposed to lead but I did not know the difference between leading at work and leading at home. Leading at home the way that I led at work was not working and was not ever going to work. In the first years of our marriage, I ran a business. It was my job. I was the boss. People did what I asked them to do. In many ways they were serving me as my employees. At home, I was to serve Nancy. She was not my employee. She was very clear on that! I did so well leading people at work but I was failing miserably at home. No wonder she had trouble following my lead. I think as husbands, most of us do not lead well at home. If we are not leading well, how can we expect our wives to follow?

Yet, as husbands, if we lead as God wants us to in our marriages (see "Love Is Leading" above), then I believe our wives will find it easy to follow our lead. It's not a men versus women thing. It's a men *and* women thing. One is no better than the other. One is no more important than the other. It is a husband and wife playing on the same team and both have equal value to the team.

For us, it was figuring out how to do this in the first half of our marriage and really living it out in the second half. Guess what? God's plan really works!

If I serve Nancy, if she knows that I pray for God's wisdom and guidance as a husband, if I listen to her and value her, then it is pretty easy for her to trust me and to follow my lead. I know you guys were hoping to get a break here but your wife's following is in response to your leading. Lead poorly and no one follows. Lead well and you will be amazed at the change in your wife.

Okay, ladies, you do not get completely off the hook here. Pray for your husband as he leads. Speak into his leadership. Tell him how well he is doing. Pray for God to mold you into the wife your husband needs. It is all part of following the leader God gave you.

Questions for You:

- When is it easiest to follow your husband's lead?
- When is it most difficult?
- How can you work as a team to be a better leader and a better follower?

Nancy: If a man is a good leader, a good mate, and his wife can trust his decisions, she's more apt to follow his lead. I think you've been a good spiritual leader in our home. I've shared in that responsibility, but I think that your strength in leadership is more in the faith part of our marriage. Also in handling our finances. A lot of women are very adept in finances, but I'm not. So I defer to you in that. I give my input, but you're more the expert. And you defer to me in certain respects. You get my input and you value it.

Dr. Kim: I especially value your knowledge from your business, and that you know much more than I do about anything to do with homes or real estate. Have there been times when it's been hard to follow me?

Nancy: Yes. I think early in our marriage you were trying to be dominant. You were domineering and I rebelled. But I've learned through the years to respect you. With that respect has come more of a willingness to lead with you and follow your lead.

Dr. Kim: So early on, when I didn't lead well and it was hard to follow, how did you handle that?

Nancy: I rebelled. I would do my own thing. It was very combative in our relationship, and we were at odds with each other a lot. There was a lot of stress.

Dr. Kim: Any particular instance?

Nancy: I think you just tried to control me in most ways.

Dr. Kim: I did. I thought I knew best and had the answers. There were things I probably did say that were best, but because of the way I did it, you pushed away from me.

Nancy: I think I learned to respect you eventually.

3. Love Is Listening

If you read my books or blogs, listen to my podcasts or follow me on social media, you know how important I think listening is in marriage. I do not think you can have an awesome marriage if you do not both listen well to each other. That is a pretty strong statement but I really believe it is true.

If 97 percent of couples that say they communicate well also say they have a good marriage, and if the most important part of communication is listening, then listening well is essential to the health of your marriage. I don't think listening well comes easy for most of us. We have to first value listening and then be very intentional in developing that skill.

Listening is not the same as hearing. When I write, I usually have background music playing. Do I hear the music? Yes. Am I really listening to it? No. I usually know when Nancy is talking to me. It is then that I have to make a choice. I can choose to hear her, which means that I kind of listen to the words—at least, well enough to know when to nod my head or say something affirmative. I can get by with that, at least for a while, but does it connect us? Does it give us what I want in our marriage? No and no.

When Nancy is talking, I want to choose to listen to her. That means I eliminate all distractions as best I can. I look her in the eyes. I focus on what she is saying so I can respond appropriately. Listening connects us and gives us what we both want in our marriage. It tells her that I love her and that what she says is important to me. It goes both ways. She has the same choices, to just hear or to really listen.

Questions for You:

- How well do you listen to each other?
- Do you listen better today in the second half than you did in the first half? Why or why not?
- How do you know if your spouse is listening to you?
- How do they know if you are listening to them?

Listening to our spouse well seems to have a really positive effect on a marriage. If you give yourselves a good grade on listening today, keep it up. If your listening needs work, make it a priority. Not only does it show love, but it sets the stage for your love to grow as you listen well to each other.

Dr. Kim: So when does the best listening happen in our marriage?

Nancy: It's usually when we're not distracted by other things. We're one on one. You've talked about how we value our time together daily, and we try to do that more on the weekends. Communication in that way where we try to put everything else aside and just talk with one another—it's really hard. I know because I have friends whose husbands are like hermits—they just won't talk. It's so frustrating for them! I think that's a huge problem in marriages. But I was gifted with a man who really knows how to communicate.

Dr. Kim: It's something we work with a lot in counseling—trying to help a man communicate in a way that can connect with his wife. A guy can say 10, 20 words and think he's communicated, but his wife needs him to connect with his emotions. A lot of times that's hard for guys.

Nancy: I think a lot of guys could use some help in that. Most women—not all, but most—can talk with their husband about what concerns them, what gives them pleasure, and so on. But men need to really learn that.

Dr. Kim: Just take the risk. Once they see how it really connects you as a couple, it's worth it.

Nancy: Some people get into excuses and say, "That's just me. I've always been quiet. I'm not a good communicator." But if you really want your marriage to get better, you need to work on it. Seriously. We can't just fall back on thinking we can't change because of the way we were raised or what we're used to.

Dr. Kim: I think that's important. A lot of what makes our communication good is a result of both of us respecting each other. I think that helps us to listen to each other. We've learned to value what each other says and to listen. I don't just think, *As soon as she quits talking here's what I'm going to say*, but I really listen to you—thanking God for you. To me it's an attitude of how I look at you and treat you. I'm not perfect at it, but in my heart it is how I feel about you, and I try to convey that through my words.

4. Love Is Cherishing

It's funny how a song can influence us. Some influence us for good and others not so much. When Nancy and I were in college, there was a song that she really liked. It was titled "Cherish" and was by a group called The Association. We listened to it together a lot.

The other day we were driving and listening to "'60s on Six" on Sirius/XM. Guess what song came on the radio? "Cherish." We sang along together and never missed a word.

Later it got me thinking. That song really impacted me. The lyrics said what was in my heart for Nancy. I wanted that in a relationship and she did too. There is something special about cherishing someone and wanting to be cherished by them in return. It conveys gentleness, kindness, and peacefulness. Here are a few of the words in the song:

> *Cherish is the word I use to describe*
> *All the feeling that I have*
> *Hiding here for you inside*
>
> *You don't know how many times*
> *I've wished that I had told you*
> *You don't know how many times*
> *I've wished that I could hold you*
> *You don't know how many times*
> *I've wished that I could*
> *Mold you into someone who could*

Cherish me as much as I cherish you

Maybe God used that song in our relationship. He can use anything, you know! The song at the very least planted the word "cherish" in my mind. I have wanted this in our marriage since the beginning. Nancy has too. It is a mindset that is fulfilled in words, actions, and behaviors. It is being eternally grateful for the gift of your spouse in marriage.

When God puts two people together in marriage, we are to embrace that gift and are also accountable to Him in how we handle that gift. Maybe "cherishing" is a new thought for you concerning your marriage. If it is, do you see value in building this in your marriage? Maybe you see it in your marriage today but you just never put a label on it before.

Here are some ways to cherish each other:

- See your spouse as a gift from God. Don't ever lose sight of that truth.
- Each day, thank God for your gift. Ask Him to guide you in your role as a husband or a wife.
- Pray each day to see your spouse through God's eyes.
- When you feel cherished by your spouse, thank them.
- Let your spouse know how much he or she means to you with your words and your actions.
- Surprise each other with something special at unexpected moments.
- Say "I love you" to each other every day.

Nancy and I were sitting outside on our patio side by side on a loveseat the other night. We were doing little more than just sitting close together. It was a special moment. We were cherishing each other without saying a word.

Kim: I would say I cherish you by being gentle with you, listening to you, and letting you know how thankful I am for you.

Nancy: I cherish you by just being there for you. Knowing that I want to spend time with you, I want to listen to you and share with you. I want to provide for and serve you. I have to stop sometimes and think about what I'm doing sometimes to make sure I'm continuing to do things to cherish you and make sure you're secure in daily knowing that I do cherish you.

God's Blueprint for Your Love

You have heard this next part before. Most of you have heard it a number of times. Most of us will hear it again. For me, it's one of those things that I have heard so often that I can tune it out without even knowing it. Yet, if you are looking for a blueprint for love in your marriage, this is it. Don't skip over this. Don't say to yourself, "I've heard all this before. Why is he taking up good space with this?" Bear with me and I promise to give you a new look at this.

If you were betting on what I think God's blueprint for love is, what would you bet on? The odds would weigh heavy on 1 Corinthians 13. If you placed your bet there, you would have won but probably not much. It's not like it was a long shot! What's the new look I promised? It's simply this. Instead of reading the word "love" as it repeats in the passage, I want you to put your name in its place.

Here is what it looks like with my name in verses 4-7 in *The Message* translation:

> ***Kim** never gives up. **Kim** cares more for others than for himself. **Kim** doesn't want what he doesn't have. **Kim** doesn't*

> *strut,* ***Kim*** *doesn't have a swelled head,* ***Kim*** *doesn't force himself on others,* ***Kim*** *isn't always "me first,"* ***Kim*** *doesn't fly off the handle,* ***Kim*** *doesn't keep score of the sins of others,* ***Kim*** *doesn't revel when others grovel,* ***Kim*** *takes pleasure in the flowering of truth,* ***Kim*** *puts up with anything,* ***Kim*** *trusts God always,* ***Kim*** *always looks for the best,* ***Kim*** *never looks back, But keeps going to the end.*

I know, it's a tall order. It also humbles me and hits me right between the eyes with my failures. Yet it is my standard. It's the blueprint that God laid out before me and you. I will never attain that standard but I will keep trying. With God's help and my perseverance, I can get a little bit closer every day. I never want to lower the standard so I can attain it. For me, I like it out of my reach. I like the small victories that I can shoot for each day. I like that I can learn from my mistakes when I fall short. I like that God has given me a map that leads to an awesome marriage.

Dr. Kim: Since God is love, how do we see love as the foundation of our marriage? How do we express it at its deepest and most intimate level?

Nancy: It's mainly all of the things we've talked about. The way we communicate. The example to our kids and to the world. Having a sure foundation.

Dr. Kim: As we've learned more about how God loves us, and been able to accept that in our own lives and in our marriage, I think we've tried to convey that to each other. It's kind of like God's love is such an integral part of our marriage, so we want to love each other the way God loves us. It's hard sometimes. The unconditional part of it is not always easy. But I think we've learned a lot about the sacrificial part of it, learning to set "self" aside for each other.

Nancy: Yes. You know it says in the Bible we're to have the same attitude as Christ, which means servanthood. I think that springs from having God as our foundation. It's all about attitude.

Dr. Kim: So how do we express love at its deepest and most intimate?

Nancy: I think through *dod* (the mingling of souls), which includes the spiritual as well as the emotional, mental, and physical. And I feel an expression of love with you when we're worshiping together.

Dr. Kim: I think where I see it a lot is when we're not even saying words but we're together and express that love.

Nancy: I think that's true. I experience a sensation of love with you without saying a word.

Dr. Kim: Sometimes we just look at each other or touch each other.

Nancy: Our conversations, our laughter, just living together.

Dr. Kim: I'm glad you brought up laughter. I think having fun together is a really intimate way we connect. We laugh at the same things, usually. You don't always like my jokes, but most of them. Then I think, continuing to work to enjoy the physical relationship, and as you've said, the *dod*, the mingling of souls. I think that's the ultimate that we experience, when our souls mingle.

Love is what it is all about. It is both the emotion and the actions. Love is the foundation of marriage. Without the foundation of love, a marriage is built on shifting sand. God is love and our relationship with Him is based on His undeserved love for us and our response to Him. Our relationship in marriage is to mirror Christ's relationship with the church. Again, it is all about love. Love at its deepest and most intimate level.

Now that we have our foundation, let's move on to intimacy and sex. Just a heads-up: they are separate for a reason. As much as culture lumps them together, we are going to define them separately. Are you ready? Let's dive into intimacy.

Part Two

Intimacy

Just What Is Intimacy?

Often when I am talking with couples, I notice they use the words "intimacy" and "sex" interchangeably. As a counselor, I have done the same thing in the past. But intimacy and sex are not the same thing. I needed to learn to communicate that distinction clearly if I was to expect couples to understand the differences.

Intimacy can certainly lead to sex but it can stand on its own as something that a couple enjoys and that draws them closer together. Communication can be intimate. Praying together can be intimate. Experiencing something special between the two of you can be intimate. Treating each other gently can be intimate. The marriage relationship is designed to give the opportunity to be as close as two people can be. Over the course of a marriage, intimacy is designed to build and grow. A couple's care for each other grows and they grow increasingly closer to each other.

In our marriage, it took us a while to figure this out. At 22, I was focused on perfecting our sex life and had no idea that things like good communication and quality time played a part. Sex without intimacy is just that—sex. Sex with intimacy is different. It's that connection at the deepest level of our souls. It's the physical, mental, emotional, and spiritual all coming together in the sex act. Any two people can experience fireworks in the sex act. When there is intimacy, it's like the two of you are surrounded by fireworks that ignite your souls in a way that words cannot describe. We will talk about the "fireworks" a lot more in Part Three of this book.

In our marriage, I think Nancy and I just stumbled into the value of intimacy. We began to put the pieces together. The more we put each other first, only behind God, the better our marriage was. Our connection to each other got better and better. On the other hand, it seemed that we could take big steps backward when our connection was struggling or missing. This thing we stumbled into could be fleeting. If we wanted intimacy to be a daily part of our marriage, it was going to take a lot more than a stumble to make it happen; it was going to take intentionality.

The first time I heard someone refer to being intentional in marriage, it got my attention. It was like discovering the cheat code for a video game. It was the answer I hadn't realized I was looking for. Being intentional was doing something on purpose. Being intentional in my marriage was me doing what I was supposed to do as a husband on purpose every single day. Finally, I had a game plan. Now the question was whether I would execute it or not.

Intimacy Defined

Dr. Kim: So how do you define intimacy?

Nancy: It's the deep connection that you can have with another person. It takes you beyond the superficial and into a deep personal relationship.

Dr. Kim: I agree. I think it connects you at a deeper level. You can connect in a lot of different ways but this one is something deeper. How has our intimacy grown over the years?

Nancy: Well, we started out very superficial. We were all about the physical. We did have a good friendship and that grew deeper as we got to know each other. Over the years, it's just grown deeper each year.

You always hear people say, "If you hang in there, the beauty will come in a marriage." It does come as you grow. You can't do it any other way than time. It is trial and error at first and then you find something that works and you stick with it, and over time it grows into a godly intimacy.

Dr. Kim: Yes, I think that's true. I think it has grown, like you said, as we've gotten to know each other better. We were always pretty honest with each other, but I think we became more transparent. I think as we connected more with God through prayer and as our intimacy with God got better, it spilled over into our marriage.

Nancy: Yes, it does. As you deepen your intimacy with God, it makes you a better Christian, a better person, a better human being, a better spouse.

Dr. Kim: Thinking of intimacy with God helps me to think of intimacy separately from the sexual piece. So I think, *Okay, what makes me intimate with God?* Well, it's spending time with Him. It's understanding Him, or trying to understand Him, though I'll never fully understand Him. It's seeing how He cares about me. Then if you put that in a marriage relationship, you can begin to develop the intimacy that you want and that God wants you to have in a marriage.

Nancy: Yes, I think a big part of intimacy both with God and in marriage is listening and being quiet and just listening to what God has to say or what your mate has to say. Quit thinking about other things and allow them to have your full attention. Just open your mind and heart to everything they're trying to say to you.

Dr. Kim: Yes, because I think, in our culture today, most people don't get listened to very much. A boss tells you what to do and you do it. So you listen to them to do the job.

But when we have someone who is going to really listen to whatever we say, whether it's something deep or not, having someone to listen to you makes a difference. It's just like we know that God listens to us and hears every prayer.

Nancy: Right.

Dr. Kim: What has hurt our intimacy?

Nancy: Not spending enough time together. Letting pride or selfishness get in the way of quality time with you.

Dr. Kim: Yes, I think you're right, especially since your love language is quality time. When we don't have that, I can just feel it. It doesn't affect me quite like it does you, but it does affect me. I think because that's your love language, it really affects you.

Nancy: Oh, absolutely.

Dr. Kim: Can you think of anything else that hurts our intimacy?

Nancy: I think when I let the everyday cares of life jump in and take over my thoughts, attitude, and mood. I'll have a bad day, or an irritating day, and that pretty much turns me off to life. That's when I need to come back and calm myself before God, listen to Him, and let Him minister to me, to get me back on track.

Dr. Kim: Yes, I agree. Another thing is when I get selfish. When I get tied up in myself or in what I'm doing, I might get short or impatient with you. What I've learned is that I've got to put you ahead of whatever else it is. Sometimes that's really easy to do and sometimes it's harder. I think you've learned that when I'm writing, or studying, or something like that, you give me grace and time to do that; and I've learned that if you do interrupt me, it's something important to you.

Nancy: Usually.

Dr. Kim: Not always?

Nancy: No.

Dr. Kim: Sometimes you just want to be with me?

Nancy: Yes.

Dr. Kim: Like when you come and sit on my lap?

Nancy: Yes.

Dr. Kim: That's good. So what grows our intimacy?

Nancy: For us, it takes spending time together every day and listening to each other. Not so much talking, which I've learned over the years. I was a talker but I really enjoy being a listener more now.

On a bigger scale, we noticed that this summer when we realized we just needed to get away from everything and go somewhere where we could be alone together. That's when we went to the beach and stayed four or five days and ended up being able to reconnect without any distractions. I think it's like instead of filling up your car with just a few gallons at a time, it's going in for the full refuel.

Dr. Kim: Yes. And I think we refuel better when we're in a place like a beach, when there's really nothing else to do. We hang out together, we eat, and we enjoy each other, and we spend all that time together. I like to go to places that are new and see new things, but for us, connecting and growing our intimacy come when it's just us. You grew up going to the beach, and it's something I've learned to love over the years.

Nancy: I've got friends who love to go to the mountains and find that peace and tranquility there. I think everybody just needs to find a spot. It may not be leaving your town; maybe it's a park or a special restaurant where you can have a quiet little booth.

Dr. Kim: Sure. Those are great short ones. I think we all need that longer period of time too.

Nancy: Yes, we do. Everybody can't do that all the time but hopefully you can get away for maybe a night or two.

Dr. Kim: Yes, we've done a lot of bed and breakfast inns in the past, or there's a little cabin we used to go to down in the mountains in southeast Oklahoma. We loved it and it was great and it was inexpensive to rent that for a few days and just be in nature and walk and enjoy each other that way. I think those are important. I think those are things that really have grown our intimacy over the years.

Nancy: Mm-hmm, I agree.

Questions for You:

- How would you define intimacy for your marriage?
- How would you rate the intimacy in your marriage today on a 1 to 10 scale, with 10 being outstanding?
- What does being intentional in your marriage look like to each of you?
- Is anything getting in the way of intimacy in your marriage today?

Five Types of Intimacy in Marriage

No matter how you rated the intimacy in your marriage today, keep reading! If it rates high, let's unpack that and look at ways to maintain and to grow your intimacy. If you rated it low or moderate, now is the time to move up the scale. What one couple describes as important to building intimacy in their marriage may differ from what another couple might say. Each and every couple is unique and their definition of intimacy will be unique too. Let's define a few of the different types of intimacy and look at how they benefit a marriage.

1. Emotional Intimacy

How comfortable are you and your spouse with each other? Are there any walls between the two of you? Is your spouse the first person you go to when you have something to share? Does your spouse know you want to hear what they have to say? Most of us married our spouse with the idea that they would be our best friend for life. They would be our first "go to" and we would be theirs. Certainly friends can fill that role but it will damage the intimacy in our marriage if our spouse is on the outside looking in.

At times, we will all have things we want to share that will be hard to share. We want to know that if we share them we will not be judged. When I share something very private or personal with Nancy, I know she will listen and that she will come alongside me in support. I do the same for her. That is emotional intimacy. For us, it took trial and error as we worked out how to be safe places for each other so that emotional intimacy could grow. Sometimes we really nailed it and sometimes we did not. Yet, even when we did not, we learned from those times, because we saw we were pushing what we wanted most in our marriage out of reach. We saw that being a safe place for each other to share meant growing closer emotionally.

In Genesis the Bible tells us that after Adam and Eve were created, they were "naked and unashamed" together (Genesis

2:25). I believe that in marriage we should be able to experience that with each other—both literally and figuratively! To me "naked and unashamed" takes real vulnerability. What's the key to great vulnerability? Safety is key. In order for your spouse to feel comfortable sharing anything with you and to truly feel open to vulnerability, you need to be a safe place for them. It's making sure your spouse knows you love and accept them completely, just as they are.

In the early years of our marriage, we did share very honestly and openly with each other. Our problem was that we did not always receive well what the other shared. We were still trying to change each other. Once we were able to set that aside and really accept the other, our sharing with each other led to greater intimacy. God helped us learn to value each other's differences. That was a huge turning point for us and it created that safe place in our marriage that both of us wanted. It was a process of continuing to learn more about each other. God is very patient with us.

On day one of our marriage, I thought I knew just about everything there was to know about Nancy, and she felt the same about me. We both probably knew only about 10 percent. Today we are closer to 100 percent. How did we get there? It was a combination of shared life experiences and lots of talking. The more things we have gone through together and the more we learned about how early life experiences shaped us, the more we have connected. Probably the real turning point was when we stopped trying to change each other and left that in God's hands. He has done a much better job than we did! Embracing each other "naked and unashamed" took our emotional intimacy way up the scale.

Dr. Kim: How do you define emotional intimacy in our marriage?

Nancy: Emotional intimacy is when you have someone you can open up to without judgment; you know you can trust them completely. You know that they care, that they love you and will do everything they can to walk with you through both the bad and good things. If it's good, you can rejoice in it together.

Dr. Kim: Yes, I think it is because we have all of those emotions, and as a counselor, it's so much better when we're able to process those and get those out. The person I think God gave us first to do that with, besides Him, is our spouse.

Nancy: Yes, and like you said, you get to provide that in a professional setting for people, which people need. A lot of times, there are people who just don't have someone like that. I think they could if they looked hard enough, but some spouses just aren't emotionally available.

Dr. Kim: If I couldn't be totally transparent emotionally with you, it'd be hard, and I think it's harder for guys. We need somebody, and we usually don't have a lot of safe people. Women do a better job of that in a lot of ways.

Nancy: I think a lot of men are beginning to see the value. I don't know if it was the pandemic or what, but it seems to me men are being more open now. They're sharing their feelings openly more, and I think that's so valuable to be transparent with people. You need one or two people that you can just open your heart to and find a way to release either the joyful or painful emotions.

Dr. Kim: Yes, and when we've had difficult times, certainly like when each of our parents died, we really did a good job of coming alongside each other and being there for each other. It's not that we had any magical wands. I can remember when my dad died and I was just lying on the bed. You didn't do anything but come and lie beside me and put your arm around me, and that was so comforting. We were connecting emotionally without saying anything.

Nancy: Exactly.

Dr. Kim: How does that differ today from the early years of our marriage?

Nancy: Oh, my gosh, we were such messes. I was just a bottle of emotions, and selfishness, and pride, and thank God we've come through that. We're never going to be perfect until we meet Jesus face to face. It was a matter of struggling through it and finding the way, and being willing to make changes, and do the things you need to do to grow in that intimacy.

Dr. Kim: Yes, I think when we were younger, obviously we had a lot of immaturity. I mean, you weren't even out of college, I'd just graduated from college. We still had all the emotional immaturity that you have in your teens and early 20s. We were trying to be married and figure out what marriage was all about. But I think you're right, over the length of our marriage, as we've gotten closer together, we've allowed ourselves to go deeper with emotional intimacy and connect on a deeper level.

Nancy: Right.

Dr. Kim: What does "naked and unashamed" mean to you in our marriage?

Nancy: Well, I mean, obviously it could mean physical. But I think it just means naked emotions. Here I am. I'm an open book. I want to share my life with you, my feelings, my physicality, everything. I just want to become one with you.

Dr. Kim: Yes, and I always think of Adam and Eve's relationship. I talk about it a lot because it impacts me so much to think about what they had with God. They were totally transparent, they could talk about anything, and God set the example for them because He accepted them. Then they sinned and things changed.

But up to that point, it was the perfect relationship. I think that, to me, "naked and unashamed" means that I can be transparent with you. I can say anything and you're not going to condemn me or look down on me for it—except some of my jokes. But with those I don't expect you to accept all of them. So I think it's just knowing that I'm totally safe with you, all the time.

Do you think it was a progression for us, or was there anything you can think of that really made a difference as we learned how to be more emotionally connected with each other?

Nancy: Well, I think that when we've had some health problems, that were pretty serious, I think that's when we really saw that the other person was there at a crucial time. That really grew us.

Dr. Kim: I agree, and I think that also, when you think that you might lose your spouse, it puts things in a different perspective.

Nancy: Yes, exactly.

Dr. Kim: You value them more. The first time you were really sick, we had been married about 16 years, something like that. Our kids were little. You were in the hospital for 17 days, and you kept getting worse. I really had a long time there to face what would it be like if you didn't get well, if you didn't come out of that.

Nancy: Well, nobody has tomorrow guaranteed. So, obviously, as we've grown older, we go, "Well, we're on the home slide, probably." But that definitely brings it into focus. If you can realize that someone could be taken from you at any time, you want to make sure you've lived every moment with them to the best.

Dr. Kim: Yes, you don't want to waste a day. I think it became more and more clear to us over time how important it is that we connect every day.

Nancy: Exactly.

Questions for You:

- How do you rate the emotional intimacy in your marriage today?
- What does "naked and unashamed" mean to you in your marriage?
- On a scale of 1-10 with 10 being incredibly safe, how much of a safe space do you feel your spouse is?
- What do you need from your spouse in order to feel safe sharing anything with them?

2. Intellectual Intimacy

The first time I heard the words "intellectual intimacy," I thought, *I'll pass on that.* I didn't go to Harvard (even though I do have a Harvard T-shirt). I did not see myself as an intellectual. I think I am pretty smart, but "intellectual" is a stretch. So when I realized just what intellectual intimacy was all about, I gave myself a break. Intellectual intimacy has nothing to do with intelligence and a lot to do with being diligent in getting to know how your spouse's mind actually works. It comes from sharing ideas, thoughts, hopes, passions, and fears with each other and having conversations that go below the surface. It comes from staying up late or even all night talking about life, marriage, and a myriad of other things. It is feeling free to share thoughts and ideas even when you know your spouse may look at things differently.

Overall, Nancy and I have done this pretty well. One of the things Nancy always said that attracted her to me was that I would talk with her. I was comfortable talking about anything and I loved talking and listening to her. When we were at TCU, there was a small Italian restaurant that we loved. We always sat in a booth and there were doors on the booth that we could close for privacy. We spent hours in our booth developing our intellectual intimacy!

I talk a lot about how important it is to be a student of your spouse. There are always things to learn about your spouse. We all change and learn and grow. The Nancy that I married is not the Nancy of today. Sure, there are some things that are the same, but she was 18 when I met her. We both had life experiences at that stage of life, but 50 years later we both have added a lot more life experiences. We have grown, matured, and learned so much. God has shaped and sanctified us.

I do not think you can learn everything there is to know about your spouse in a lifetime. I think that most of us just get lazy and stop studying. It takes effort to study your spouse, but there is a big payoff for all the effort. Life continues to be fun and interesting and challenging and awesome.

I believe that one of God's plans for marriage is embodied in this verse from Proverbs 27:17: "As iron sharpens iron, so one person sharpens another." God has used Nancy in my life in so many ways. There is no way I would be who I am today without her. She encourages me, listens to me, tells me when I am wrong in a loving way, and challenges me. All that goes into our intellectual intimacy.

Let's look at how we can intentionally build intellectual intimacy into our marriage.

When we were first married, we had not developed a lot of activities to do together. When we were dating, our activities revolved around dates. Those consisted of going to movies, going to parties, going to dinner, and hanging out. Once we were married Nancy was living in a new city and finishing college at a new school. I was trying to start a career. Our lives were busy and we were getting into a rut during our first year of marriage. We needed new things to do together. We needed to be intentional about time spent together and shared experiences, because it wasn't happening by accident.

We tried golf but that failed for a thousand reasons. We tried tennis and found something we both liked. However, our competitiveness kept us from playing each other, except when practicing. It was amazing how intense we could get with each other when on different sides of the net. The best activities for us have been ones that were not competitive. We could not even play backgammon without getting riled at each other! Through lots of trial and error, we have discovered so many things we really enjoy doing together today, including cooking, gardening, hiking, exploring, watching British mysteries, playing pickleball, and sharing books.

Having these shared interests and intentional time together strengthens our intellectual intimacy because not only does it give us opportunities to talk as we do these things together, but it also gives us lots of things to talk about when we intentionally share an interest together.

If you are doing well in this area, keep it up. If not, each of you write down five things you would like to do together. Then try them out one at a time, alternating lists. Give each one a chance and see what you can come up with.

Some couples seem to do this easily, while others struggle. Sometimes when I suggest to a couple that they need to spend time together, just the two of them, they look almost frightened. If you are on the "we struggle" side, try this: get your feet wet. Set aside 15 minutes every day as uninterrupted time for the two of you to talk. Share about your day, how you saw God in the world today, your hopes, your dreams, or something funny. It may be awkward at first but keep it up.

Another thing that I think helps but see very few couples do is asking each other's opinion on things. Maybe you are re-covering a sofa and never thought to ask your spouse's opinion on the fabric before. Ask. Not because you have to, but because you want to value their opinion and you want to know what they like and dislike.

My hope for your intellectual intimacy is this: There is nothing that you would not talk about or share with your spouse, and you do this in complete confidence and with absolutely no fear. You are willing to try new things together. You develop interests together. Your values are in alignment. You always have each other's back. You find creative ways to connect every day. That's it!

Dr. Kim: What has intellectual intimacy looked like for us over the years?

Nancy: For us? Well, again, we were not being very intellectual when we started out. But over the years we talked at length about different situations. When we had young kids, we talked about what they were going through and what we were going through, and we learned how to parent during that time. That grew us at the intellectual level. Sometimes we both read the same book or we discuss social issues, political issues, and we do that with friends. But we do that on a one-on-one basis quite a bit, and it's just another layer of intimacy that is crucial.

Dr. Kim: Yes, and I think we value each other. If I ask you a question about something, maybe it is political or something like that. Even if you give me an answer that's different from what I'm thinking, I'll listen and value it.

Nancy: Well, yes, and we can debate each other and that's healthy, as long as we don't let anger get in the way. But I think anything that can spur you on intellectually is wonderful.

Dr. Kim: And you bring up things sometimes that I haven't thought of that may make me look at things differently or add a new perspective. So I think we're good, and I think it's valuable because I trust you and you trust me. We listen to each other and we don't just blow each other off. I've worked with couples where one will say something and the other person just acts like they didn't even say it.

That's not healthy and it doesn't show value for that person. If that continues, they're going to shut down at some point. I think we've kept that door open and we're better because of it.

Nancy: I think it's exciting to have intellectual interests, and there are so many ways to do that now. If there's something you want to learn more about, you can just google it. I love to do that and share it with you, and I know it deepens our relationship.

Dr. Kim: It lets us know what the other person is thinking and what's important to them and what they're looking at and thinking about, or what they are trying to figure out.

Nancy: It makes me a better person when I hear what you have to say and vice versa.

Dr. Kim: Yes, absolutely. What is your favorite way of connecting with me intellectually?

Nancy: I love when we watch and discuss the Bible Project in the evenings. It's pretty exciting.

Dr. Kim: I'm glad you brought that up because I think that has been something that we have grown in together. We've read through the Bible together every year for a number of years, yet we've both learned and grown through the Bible Project and their videos and the way they dissect the books of the Bible.

Nancy: Exactly. I have a friend who loves to listen to a sermon together with her husband each week. They really enjoy it and they spend the whole evening talking about the subject of the pastor's message.

Dr. Kim: That's a good point you brought up, because with technology now, if you think, *Oh, I've heard that pastor's really good*, well, you can listen to him. I hardly know any pastor who doesn't provide access to their audio online. That gives you a chance to experience things together. I remember the first Easter of the pandemic, we had all these pastors we wanted to listen to. I think we listened to six sermons that day. It was cool.

Nancy: It was.

Dr. Kim: We look for those opportunities to grow together. I listen to a lot of books and a lot of podcasts, and I'll share things with you that I heard that day that I think you would be interested in. I think that really helps too. Is there anything that you feel uncomfortable sharing with me?

Nancy: No. Mm-mm.

Dr. Kim: Yes, I know. Same way. I'm sure there were times we held back and we were trying to figure out how to be safe with each other. But I think now I would say anything and I know that you would accept it, listen, and we could talk about it.

Nancy: Or challenge me on something.

Dr. Kim: Or you can challenge me on something.

Nancy: Well, yes.

Questions for You:

- Now that you have a definition of intellectual intimacy, how would you rate yours in your marriage on a 1 to 10 scale with 10 being awesome?
- What is a first step in strengthening or growing the intellectual intimacy in your marriage?
- If you set aside an hour for just the two of you, how would you use that time to connect intellectually?
- What activities would you put on your "I'd like to try" list?

3. Physical Intimacy

Let's define this as everything physical except sex. That would include hugs, kisses, cuddling, holding hands, hands everywhere but private parts, and whatever else you want to add that fits the definition. It is nonsexual touch. I think the problem with this is that often, women seem to enjoy it more than men. It's not that we men cannot enjoy it, but generally we would rather just bypass all of that and get to the sex. Right! Yet God gave us nonsexual touch for a reason. So let's look at it.

Before we were married I got it. Sex was to be reserved for marriage and so there needed to be boundaries for us before marriage. That was really difficult for me. I was so attracted to Nancy and honestly pushed the needle as far as I could. So when we married and could have sex anytime we wanted, I had no use for nonsexual touching. The problem I discovered was that Nancy did still see nonsexual touching as valuable. Now we had something to resolve and I was slow coming around. Through this, I learned something. All this physical intimacy that did not include sex could really be fun. Plus, when I focused on the nonsexual touching, Nancy felt like I got her and the sex improved too!

Dr. Gary Brown says, “Physical affection or intimacy through hugging, kissing, and touching is just as crucial in the development of relationship bonds as communication.” I believe a relationship must have physical intimacy to survive. Without it, something is missing, and it is something important. God created us with these touch receptors all over our bodies because we need physical intimacy. Have you ever come home after a difficult day and received a big hug from your spouse? Do you remember how your mood changed? You had renewed energy after you thought your energy was gone for the day. That is exactly how God designed our bodies to work. What if on that same day you came home and had no hug? Think about how that would affect you. Instead of feeling rejuvenated, you would just continue on your downward spiral. If you had a choice, which would you choose? I thought so.

There are also other consequences to a marriage without physical intimacy. You can grow apart and feel distant from each other. You may argue more. The fun may slip out of your marriage.

I see it all the time. If I am at the park people watching, it is usually pretty obvious the couples that have physical intimacy in their marriage and those that do not. The couples I see holding hands and laughing together and walking side by side so their bodies touch get it. Other couples may be walking together but with no touch and no interaction. The physical intimacy piece of their marriage is missing.

There have been some times when our physical intimacy was not the best. We never had a drought but we had some dry days. This is my experience. I did not like the dry days. I missed Nancy’s touch and it was a huge red flag to me that something needed to happen to mend our relationship. So we never went very long without physical intimacy. Without physical touch I feel like a small boat adrift without a rudder, and with it I feel anchored to my spouse and my marriage.

One thing I hear a lot in the counseling room is that women feel used by their husband if the only touch they receive is sexual, or if any fond touch is expected to turn to sex later. Our spouse needs to know we want them for who they are and not just their body. They need to know that we desire their closeness for intimacy's sake and not just sex's sake. Nonsexual touching shows this. It builds a closeness outside of sex that helps both spouses feeling cared for and valued.

I mentioned that women typically see nonsexual touching as important and men don't after marriage, but sometimes it can be the other way around. Regardless of the gender, if you aren't making nonsexual touch a priority and you don't seem to "need it" but your spouse does, you need to make a plan to make this important to you. Even if you don't "need" the nonsexual touch, your spouse does and your marriage does. Don't ignore this important way to connect and have intimacy. Start building new habits of touching your spouse with no sexual intent.

Dr. Kim: What is your favorite form of nonsexual touching?

Nancy: When you tickle my back.

Dr. Kim: It's like when we're watching TV and we're in separate chairs, and you come and squeeze down right in front of me and I know what you want. I mean, you don't have to say it, it's like, "Tickle on my back, scratch my back, rub my shoulders." Those kinds of things.

From my perspective, you have really grown in enjoying physical touch. You didn't come out of a real touchy-feely home, and I did. I think it took you a little while to really value that.

But now I think we both enjoy nonsexual physical touch with each other, and I think we see that connection. I think God created our bodies so that hugging and that kind of thing energize us. If I come home from a hard day and you give me a big hug, it's like, "Let's go! We'll conquer the world." I get energy.

Nancy: Yes, and plus, you're warm.

Dr. Kim: Yes, that helps a lot, doesn't it?

Nancy: It helps a ton.

Dr. Kim: Yes, because you kind of wear me when you're in bed with me. You get as close as you can, especially in the winter, or if we've got the AC down really cold.

So why is nonsexual touch important to you and to our marriage?

Nancy: I used to think the nonsexual touching was just your way of getting to the sexual touching.

Dr. Kim: You were probably right most of the time. Like when I would rub your back so we could have sex.

Nancy: Exactly. Now I can feel more comfortable knowing that you can just tickle my back.

Dr. Kim: Yes, and I think that's something I've had to work on because I'm attracted to you. If I was rubbing your back, it was easy to let my mind go to other places. Now I think you've taught me how to really enjoy that nonsexual touch because you enjoy it. I know I can make you happy by doing those things. I think we've grown in that too.

Nancy: You also enjoy me reaching over and rubbing your neck when we're in the car.

Dr. Kim: Absolutely, I love it. I love it when we're just lying in bed and you rub the back of my neck, or my hair, or something like that. One thing that I like that you've become so much better at is holding hands. You've never really been a big hand holder.

Nancy: I'm still not a big hand holder.

Dr. Kim: But sometimes you'll reach over and grab my hand. That means a lot because that was something that I saw my parents do. As I was growing up, my parents held hands all the time when they walked. So I think, for me, that was something that you were "supposed to" do in marriage. I know that it's not a "supposed to" but I think it's something that I enjoy.

Can you think of a time, in our marriage, when we did not have physical intimacy?

Nancy: Well, yes, I can think of times when we didn't and we got on each other's nerves more. We would get testy with each other.

Dr. Kim: Yes, we needed that hug, kiss connection, something like that, just that touch. God made our bodies that way, so we're supposed to touch. You're not supposed to live with your spouse without touching.

Nancy: Exactly.

Dr. Kim: I think for guys, we've got to learn how to enjoy nonsexual touching. It's not just to pacify our wife so we can get to something else, but to learn to really enjoy it.

Nancy: You have come a long way!

Questions for You:

- How do you define physical intimacy in your marriage?
- What can each of you do to grow this area of your marriage?
- What are the benefits for the two of you in keeping physical intimacy a priority in your marriage?

4. Experiential Intimacy

Have you ever had an awesome experience without your spouse? Then did you feel frustrated as you tried to describe the experience to your spouse? There just weren't words to describe what you experienced to someone who was not there. When we experience things together that we both enjoy, we have experiential intimacy. It's not about words or thoughts or feelings; it's about the experience.

Nancy and I can enjoy watching a movie together and enjoy the shared experience. We recently finished watching an eight-part streaming series that we loved. While we were watching, we never really said much to each other but would occasionally look at each other and say, "What do you think is going to happen?" Then at the end of each episode we would usually both say, "This is so good." We were connecting through the experience.

The same thing can happen when we go to a game. We are big OKC Thunder fans and have experienced so many great last-second wins together. We share the excitement. It's experiential intimacy. The same thing happens when we watch our grandkids play sports. The best is the experience we have together at church. There is nothing like worshiping together with Nancy. I feel close to God and to her. As important as the emotional intimacy, physical intimacy, and intellectual intimacy are to a marriage, experiential intimacy may be my favorite. It usually takes the least effort and can produce amazing intimacy.

Nancy and I grew up in very different homes but each of us grew to really love each other's parents. Nancy's mom died the year we celebrated our sixteenth anniversary. She fought an amazing 13-year battle with cancer. She was one of the strongest women I ever knew. The morning she died, I was at the counseling center where I was on staff. One of Nancy's sisters called me with the news. I often take our modern technology for granted until I remember the old days before cell phones. This happened in the old days, so I had to drive to Nancy to tell her; besides I wanted to tell her face to face. I jumped in my old van and headed to her office. I was a wreck. Partly because I loved her mom, but also because I wasn't sure how to tell Nancy or what to do. So I cried and prayed all the way to her office.

I must have looked like a mess when I stepped into her office. Her boss was there and I whispered, "Where's Nancy? Her mom just died." She was so kind. She put me in an empty office, got Nancy, and left us alone. The next few days were a blur. We packed, picked the kids up from school, and headed to Houston. It was not until after we got back home to Oklahoma City that we both realized we felt closer to each other because of the experience. I did not have any great words for her. I was just there and never left her side. I think that was the first time I really understood what experiential intimacy was all about. Over the next 21 years, we experienced the deaths of both my parents and her dad. Each one drew us closer together. We were there for each other and that was more than enough.

There have been so many of these experiences over the years. Holding our son and then our daughter for the first time. Then the same with our grandchildren. Experiencing and celebrating God's blessings and His goodness. Christmas mornings and

Easter Sundays. Milestone events for our family together and as individuals.

In 1998, Nancy woke me up in the middle of the night in pain. She thought it was her gallbladder. When the pain had started the day before, she called her doctor, who told her to come in the next day. By evening the pain was better and by bedtime she felt pretty good. Now the pain was back. I wanted to take her to the ER but she wanted to wait, so I rubbed her back and she went back to sleep. About 5 a.m., she woke me and said, "I think we need to go to the hospital." It was a short drive to the hospital and I let her out at the ER entrance while I went to park the car.

When I walked into the hospital, I did not see Nancy. The nurse said, "They took her back to a room," and led me to it. I walked in and there were at least three people around her. She was hooked up to all kinds of equipment. My heart was beating out of my chest. The doctor turned to me and said, "Your wife is having a heart attack. I have called a cardiologist and we are taking her into surgery." I'm pretty good with doctors and hospitals and blood—unless Nancy is involved. Then I lose it. Apparently, I turned pale and a nurse caught me and lowered me into a chair. It was pretty embarrassing. My wife is having a heart attack and one of the nurses has to come over and take care of her wimpy husband. The nurse said all the right things but I knew I would be a story at the morning coffee break, and I wouldn't blame her.

The next few hours were tense. Nancy was in surgery. I was trying to stay positive. The kids were both away at college. Finally, a young doctor came out looking for me: Nancy was okay. There was some damage but he hoped with time it would heal itself. He let me go in to see her. She was groggy but she was there and she was alive. They kept her for a few days, first in ICU and then in a regular room. Bringing her home was one of the best days of my life. This experience did so much for our marriage. It helped us both see how fragile life is and how quickly things can change. We went through the same experience but from entirely different perspectives, yet the experiential intimacy was off the charts.

Experiential intimacy is not something you can totally manufacture. Sure, you can watch a movie together, but you never know going in if it will connect you or not. You can plan some experiences that you hope will connect the two of you but you can't make the intimacy happen.

This is what you can do: be by each other's side so that there are opportunities for experiential intimacy. Work hard to live life together and not lead separate lives. When hard experiences come, make sure you are by your spouse's side and on their team. Don't disappear and don't flake out on your spouse when they need you most. Be intentional to look for opportunities to share experiences, and be intentional to be on your spouse's side when the unplanned and unexpected things happen. Just like after Nancy's heart attack, even the hard and scary experiences can grow us closer in the end.

Another thing you can do is work hard on the other areas of intimacy that we've been talking about. That builds a foundation where the experiential intimacy can happen.

Dr. Kim: What normal experiences do you think connect us intimately?

Nancy: Well, I love it when you get home and we spend time together, just you and me. I think holidays and events, the things we enjoy doing together. You've made me into a real sports fan and we connect on that level now, and I think that's great.

Dr. Kim: Yes, we had a Saturday during football season when we watched most or a lot of three different games. In the early years of our marriage you probably wouldn't have done that. But we had a reason to watch them. We either wanted one team to win or the other team to lose. And all of our teams won and it was really exciting; we were both so excited. By the end of the night when the last game was over, at 11 or something, we were so hyped up, we were ready to go do something.

Nancy: Yes, that's true. Over the years, we've built traditions around things we enjoy and holidays, and stuff like that. We just really love traditions together. There's just something about history and tradition in a marriage.

Dr. Kim: Yes, I think about the years our kids were at home on Christmas Eve. After they went to bed, we always had a special time. It was just us and we would sit together and look at the Christmas tree. Sometimes we'd watch a Christmas movie or listen to music. It was just us. I remember that first year we were married. We were in our little apartment, with our little Christmas tree that we thought looked so good, that probably looked so ugly but we just loved it, and we would sit together and look at it.

Nancy: At Christmas, we've always taken a day or so to shop together for everybody.

Dr. Kim: I always look forward to that.

Nancy: Yes, we enjoy picking out stuff. But we do love holidays.

Dr. Kim: Yes, we do. And then I think we've learned to look for opportunities. Sometimes it's exploring, because we love to do that. We love to drive to different places and see things we haven't seen, or try to find old buildings, or whatever. I think just knowing that we like exploring together has given us some really good experiences.

What are some of the life experiences that have connected us?

Nancy: Tell me one of yours and then that'll get me going.

Dr. Kim: I would probably say all of our kids' and grandkids' births were really special. Seeing them for the first time, holding them for the first time. That connection and the responsibility when it was with our kids. Knowing we've got 18 years ahead of us to raise them and knowing we had to figure out how to do that. Then as grandparents there is just the joy where you just feel freer to love them and spoil them.

Nancy: You're not totally responsible for them.

Dr. Kim: Yes, I've learned that they're not as fragile as I thought they were when they were little. You just have fun with them and try to pour into them and help them to have a really good life growing up.

Nancy: Exactly. I mean that's pretty awesome. How do you top the kids and grandkids?

Dr. Kim: You don't. So what builds a foundation in our marriage for experiential intimacy to happen?

Nancy: Just being open to creating things with our family, with our friends, with yourself, with your spouse.

Dr. Kim: I think we're both willing to try new things.

Nancy: Yes.

Dr. Kim: I'm always thinking of new things. But you've always been flexible with trying new things. Then if we don't like it, we don't do it again. I think some couples go stagnant after a time and they just settle in and it's, "Oh, we'll just sit here and watch TV again."

Nancy: It's a rut. Just get out of that rut.

Dr. Kim: Yes, there's just so much to live in life and to figure out. No matter where you live, there are always things to do. I think our willingness to put ourselves in a position to have those things happen has helped a lot.

What are some of the other things that we've grown together in?

Nancy: Ministry. Like when we went on those trips with the Billy Graham Association to Amsterdam when you counseled evangelists from around the world who were attending the conference. Those were really special. Because not only were we traveling, but we were doing so for God and serving Him.

Dr. Kim: They were fabulous experiences and I think that if I'd gone by myself without you and come back, there's no way I could have ever told you my experiences in a way you could have understood. It had to be something we experienced together.

Nancy: Right.

Dr. Kim: I remember sitting in that auditorium in Amsterdam with thousands of people from all over the world, all worshiping and singing, and I thought, *This is what heaven's going to be like. All these different kinds of people are going to be there.*

Nancy: That's right. It was really special.

Dr. Kim: It was so cool. It was such a great experience.

Questions for You:

- Each of you share a time when you felt experiential intimacy with each other.
- When did an experience connect you that took you by surprise?
- What can you do to help lay the foundation for experiential intimacy in your marriage?

5. Spiritual Intimacy

Of all the different types of intimacy a couple can experience in a marriage, I believe this is the most important. In the book of Genesis, when there was just one man and just one woman, we read that they had a very special relationship with God. They spent time with God every single day. I have always thought it was interesting that in describing God's relationship with this couple, the Bible says God spent time with the two of them together. This is a picture of total spiritual intimacy, and I believe it is God's plan for every married Christian couple today. This intimacy, in my opinion, stands above all the rest. It is the essence of intimacy, and it connects a couple with each other and to the Creator of the universe. It does not get any better than that!

In our marriage, Nancy and I both have our own one-to-one relationship with God. It's how we grow individually as Christians. It's what gives each of our lives purpose. Then we have our relationship with God together as a married couple. The Bible tells us that the married relationship out of all the possible relationships in the world stands only second to our relationship with God. So together we have a relationship with God and it's just the three of us.

From our wedding night all the way to today, we have prayed together. There is nothing that has knit us closer to each other and to God than prayer. It's being in His presence together knowing that He has a plan for our marriage and that plan is good. Over the years, God has helped us raise our kids and impact our grandkids. He has given us answers that we never would have had by ourselves. He has walked us through tough times and joyful times and has never left our sides. Honestly, without Him there would not be this fifty-year marriage. We could not have done it without Him.

On our wedding night, shortly after we finally got to our hotel room after the wedding and the reception, Nancy looked at me and said, "We need to pray." For years, I thought, *I wish I was the one who had said that*, but I didn't. If I am being completely honest, praying was the last thing on my mind at that particular moment. Yet, looking back, as I have learned the importance of being a spiritual leader in our home, I wish I had been the one to say, "We need to pray." Since that night, we have prayed together about 99 percent of the days of our marriage. That's over 19,000 days!

When people ask me what has made the biggest impact on our marriage, I always say praying together. Our prayer life together has evolved over the years. We have gone from praying the Lord's Prayer each night, simply because it was a prayer we both knew, to becoming comfortable enough to pray from the heart about anything that was on our minds. The more we learned about each other and about God, the more we saw the value in prayer. When we felt afraid or exhausted or defeated or that we could not take another step forward, we prayed and God answered. He truly has never left us or forsaken us.

Reading the Bible together as a couple is another way to grow in spiritual intimacy. As we did with prayer, it also took us a long time to realize the value in reading the Bible together. The first time I read the Bible all the way through, we had been married about five years. We were about to have our first child and I knew

I needed all the guidance that I could get. Nancy had been in Bible studies with other women most of our marriage. I had not. We knew there had to be value in reading the Bible together but we just could not get it going. I was lost. Where would we start? I tried letting the Bible just fall open and then reading what was in front of us. That may work for some people but not for us. Starting in the middle of Leviticus or 1 Chronicles did not do much to encourage us to keep reading.

Then came YouVersion and the Bible app, which opened the door to the Bible for us individually and as a couple. We started reading through the Bible together every year. Through the app we could read the same verses every day either together or on our own and then connect by talking about what we read. If I learned something from the day's reading or thought God used the verses to help me, I could share that with Nancy and she could do the same with me. Then we started reading shorter plans together at night before we would pray. God spoke to us through the Word and He still does.

We were married five years before we had kids. For the first three of those years, we were the only married couple out of our friends. We were all in our early 20s and could still get into party mode. Yet, no matter what the Saturday night held for us, we were always in church on Sunday morning. It certainly was not because we were saints. In fact, we felt just the opposite. I guess we were doing self-imposed penance. We felt better after going to church.

Looking back, our motivation for being in church was not always the best but we were there and God used that to grow us closer to Him. One day we both realized that we really liked being in church and that it did make a difference in our lives. There is something special about worshiping together as a couple. You hear the same message, sing the same songs, and pray the same prayers. There have been a lot of instances and places where

Nancy and I have felt God's presence, but never do we experience it more than in church. It is the three of us again.

Lots of couples do really well in one or more of the types of intimacy that we have discussed so far. Very few couples do well with spiritual intimacy. I think there can be a number of reasons why. For instance, some people feel their spiritual life is very personal and they like it that way. It's true that it is personal, but developing spiritual intimacy together does not take away from your own spiritual life. And when we add the element of spiritual intimacy into our marriage, it can enhance our relationship with God and with our spouse. We were designed for that intimate relationship with God.

Another reason I see is that people just don't feel equipped to have a spiritual relationship together. They may feel inadequate or that they don't know enough about the Bible or that they are afraid of being that transparent with their spouse. There are probably a lot of other reasons but none of them should keep us from pursuing spiritual intimacy with our spouse. It is one of the things that I believe God wants for us. Don't forget that the very first married couple ever had God right smack in the middle of their marriage. He wanted that with them and He wants it with the two of you.

If you have a hard time knowing where to start with spiritual intimacy, I encourage you to check out the resources we have at Awesome Marriage. Our Couples' Scripture Challenge and our 15 Daily Prayers for Your Wife/Husband resources would both be great places to start. We also have dozens of marriage Bible Reading Plans on YouVersion. Simply download the YouVersion app and search "Awesome Marriage" under Plans, then choose the one that's right for you.

So much of our spiritual intimacy is difficult to explain. I think Nancy and I know that there was a time we did not have it and then we had it. We still have it today. I think we both wanted it in our marriage, but we couldn't just say, "Bring on the spiritual intimacy," and expect it to happen. It could happen that way since God can do anything but that has not been our experience. I think it happened because we prayed together, read the Bible together, and worshiped together.

There are two areas of our life together where we really feel "two become one." The first is the sexual relationship and the second is spiritual intimacy. Actually, I think that is God's plan. There is a spiritual component to sex, which we'll talk about in the next part of the book. My bottom line is this: spiritual intimacy takes consistency day after day. It is being diligent together in the things that connect us to God. If you are there, keep doing what you are doing. If you are not there yet, you can be. Seek God together and know without a doubt that He will show up big time!

Dr. Kim: Why do you think God wants spiritual intimacy for a couple?

Nancy: Well, everybody needs an individual relationship with God through Christ. But it's just profound and totally necessary in a marriage to have that as a couple. It gives you the grounding in Christ, who invented marriage. I just think it's the lifeblood of every good marriage.

Dr. Kim: Yes. Years ago a couple said something to me after I had given a talk. I was talking about the spiritual intimacy of a couple. This couple had probably been married 40 years.

They each had a really good relationship with the Lord. Yet they had never prayed together. They had never done anything like that together. And so, when they came up to talk afterward, they said, "We never thought about praying together. Thank you."

I think that goes back to Adam and Eve. They were there with God together every day. God didn't come every day and say, "Adam, I'm going to take a walk with you and bring you back and take a walk with Eve." Instead, He walked with them together.

There's something about that husband, wife, and God relationship that's very special and different than any other two-people relationship can be with God.

When do you think we nail it with spiritual intimacy?

Nancy: I think it's a combination. I think it's worshiping regularly in church together and discussing what the pastor talked about that day. And then individually, we have quiet times; in the morning and at night we have a time with God together before bed where we do the Bible Project, YouVersion plans, or other devotionals. In our small group we have a topic and we all discuss it together, and then we all go home and discuss more of it with each other. I think it's just a combination of everything.

Dr. Kim: Yes, I agree, and I think we have valued praying together our whole marriage. That has been huge for us. I don't know if we really knew what we were doing when we started praying together the very first time in marriage. But we knew it was important and we've seen the value of that over the years.

Nancy: Right, and now we don't just pray at night or in the morning. Wherever we are and we hear a need, we'll stop and pray for that person or that need.

Dr. Kim: Prayer has become a regular part of our life. If something comes up, it's just very natural now, but it didn't used to be. I think we had to get more comfortable. I had to get more comfortable with praying out loud. All those things, God grew us over the years.

For me, the time of worship in church is very special. I love that because I feel so connected to God and I feel so connected to you. And if you're not there with me, which is very seldom, I feel a void.

Nancy: Yes, me too.

Dr. Kim: So when do we fall short with spiritual intimacy?

Nancy: Well, we've really been pretty good at this, but I know we've had times when we've fallen back on it some. Times when our hearts really hadn't been into it. We might get a little legalistic about something and we just need to stop, regroup, and change what we're doing.

Dr. Kim: Yes, I think so, and I think it's easy because we know those things are important; we want to do them every day and keep doing them the rest of our marriage. So it's not just a routine that we check off but something that we embrace and grow through together.

Nancy: Right. I mean, don't become legalistic; that's key. Because that just takes away all the spontaneity and the joy.

Dr. Kim: Right, God wants us to want to spend that time with Him. And I think when you do, you see God show up, and you see Him teach you things, and you see Him answer prayers. All those things continue to grow us together. At times we have prayed for something and God has answered that prayer. And then we knew it only could have come from Him. That made such a difference.

Nancy: Exactly.

Dr. Kim: Of prayer, reading the Bible, and worshiping, which do you feel contributes the most to spiritual intimacy for us?

Nancy: Hmm, prayer.

Dr. Kim: I agree. I love the worship, but I think prayer is how God has grown us and how we've seen Him work in our prayers. And I'm so thankful that you started us on that, on our wedding night. Because if you hadn't, I don't know; I think eventually we would have, but it was that lady who mentored you who said, "You need to do this." I don't even know who she was, but I thank her for making sure that you thought of that.

Nancy: I know. It was easy for me at that time to be legalistic about my faith. She told me that she believed God would rather have you not come to Him if you were doing it out of legalism. Wait until He leads you and you come in faithfulness and love, instead of an "I have to" mentality.

Dr. Kim: Did we pray together before we got married?

Nancy: No, I don't think so.

Dr. Kim: I don't think we did. And that was never stressed to us as a couple in our premarital counseling or anything else. So, again, this lady was amazing.

Questions for You:

- On a 1 to 10 scale with 10 being the highest, rate your marriage in the areas of praying together, reading the Bible together, and worshiping together.
- If you as a couple made spiritual intimacy a goal, what would be your steps and your accountability?
- Why would God, who has access to every person in the world, want to be spiritually intimate with the two of you?

There are probably other types of intimacy, but these are my top five. As we close this section on types of intimacy and begin to look at the essentials of intimacy, let me ask you this question: If you were to rank these five types of intimacy in the order of importance to you, how would you rank them? There may be some that are easy for you and some that are difficult for you. Maybe one of them was in your marriage in the past but is no longer there today. Nancy and I value each of them.

One of the things we have learned, though, is that they each take effort. It goes back to the idea of intentionality in marriage. Great marriages don't happen by accident, and the same is true for each type of intimacy in marriage. I wish so much that once we got emotional intimacy down, it never wavered or changed. I wish that was also true with intellectual, physical, experiential, and spiritual intimacy, but it's not. They all take intentionality from the two of you every day.

Look at it this way: If you are going to put effort into something today, is there anything with a better payoff than these five areas of intimacy? Let me make a suggestion. Take these five types of intimacy and order them in the way you ranked them earlier. Now take the one that is in first place and commit to being intentional with it together each day for the next month. Then each month add another type until you have added all five. As you add each new type, keep doing what you did with the others before. Can you imagine the intimacy you will have a year from today if you do this? Each month you will experience intimacy. Each month your intimacy will grow. It is not like someone is throwing five baseballs at you all at once. They are coming in one at a time and slowly so you can catch each one and make it a part of your daily life together.

The Essentials of Intimacy

Trust

When was the first time someone broke trust with you? Who was it and what were the circumstances? Most of us are going to have a memory flash into our mind. What was yours?

The summer I turned seven, my family moved into a new house. It was bigger than our old house and I had my own new, big room. The neighborhood was full of new houses and lots of families with kids. It was not long before I had made a new best friend, and we literally played outside together from morning to night day after day. It was great. I'd never had a best friend before. We explored, we built things, and we talked about almost everything imaginable.

One day my friend told me that he thought we should become blood brothers. I liked the idea of "being brothers," but I was a little hesitant about the blood part. In the past, every time that I saw my own blood, it made me feel sick. But I couldn't tell him that, so one night we performed the ritual with a knife he borrowed from his mom's kitchen. We each cut a finger to draw blood and then put our cut fingers together. We were now officially blood brothers. My new brother then said we each needed to share a secret that no one else knew and we would keep that secret sacred and never tell anyone. It only added to the specialness of being blood brothers. I told him something I had thought I would never tell anyone—except maybe God some day. I liked this blood-brother deal.

The next morning I was greeted by my mother. She'd gotten a phone call from my "blood brother's" mother, because as soon as he got home, he told her my secret. I remember thinking that I had liked trusting him and being his blood brother, but now that was gone. I thought I would probably never trust him again.

Dr. Kim: What is your first memory of someone breaking trust with you?

Nancy: I think it was in elementary school. Probably fourth or fifth grade. My best friend had something going on with another friend of hers, and she was trying to act like she was best friends with both of us. She had a party and didn't invite me, and that was the first time that I remember just being crushed. Later on, I had a boyfriend who played around on me, and that really hurt my feelings too. That really crushed me.

Dr. Kim: How did that affect that relationship?

Nancy: Well, it made me not trust them. It made me not want to spend time with them anymore or get on a deep level with them anymore.

Dr. Kim: How did that affect you in future relationships?

Nancy: I felt like the peer pressure that I had growing up from other girls was pretty harsh. People were very sarcastic and critical, which made me feel like I had to be sarcastic and critical to survive, and it took me a long time before I could overcome that. Then after my boyfriend played around on me, it was very hard to let myself completely be vulnerable in any relationship for a long time.

Dr. Kim: I don't know if we've talked about it that much, but a couple of times, growing up, I had relationships, but they broke up and I wasn't the one who broke up, and it affected me. I put my guard up, and I think it came off as I was insecure. And maybe I was. But I just didn't want to get hurt again.

When we started dating, we had a good dating relationship. There was one time we broke up, though, and it just crushed me.

I thought, *I can't do this again.* So that was when I came and met you as you were coming out of the night class you were attending.

I don't know if you were surprised to see me or not, but we hadn't talked in a couple of days and then we talked things through and we got back together. But I think those experiences, in a bad way, made me insecure. The good thing is, it made me continue pursuing you even after we broke up.

Nancy: You just knew I was the one.

Dr. Kim: I did know you were the one.

Questions for You:

- Now go back to your memory. Who was that first person who broke trust with you?
- How did you feel?
- How did that affect you in future relationships?

Recovering After Broken Trust

I do not think that anyone would argue the fact that trust is essential to a marriage. I have never seen a healthy marriage where trust was broken again and again. Trust and marriage go hand in hand. Trust is one of the essential ingredients of an awesome marriage. There are different kinds of trust. I have counseled many couples over the years who are healing after an affair. When an affair happens, trust must be rebuilt, but it is one of the most difficult things that a spouse ever has to do.

One particular time I was counseling a couple and the husband had had an affair. As this wife was seeking to trust her husband to be faithful to her for the rest of his life, I wanted her to also see a bigger perspective. Were there areas where she did trust him? Her first response was an emphatic no. Then I asked her if she trusted him to provide. Her answer was yes. I asked her if she trusted him to be a good father, and again her answer was yes. We went on to find other ways she did trust him. Now, that did not diminish his affair or the pain it brought, but it did give her hope that trust could be rebuilt in that part of their marriage.

If this second half of your marriage is going to be everything that you want it to be, any trust issues that have built up will need to be resolved. Maybe it is something that has never been addressed. Maybe it is an issue that you tried to resolve and finally kind of gave up on. Step one is putting it on the table. That may scare you but it is the right first step. Share with your spouse what the issue is and that you want to get it resolved for both of you. Be honest. Be open. Address it as a team. As a team, you need to make your marriage the winner here, not one spouse over the other! If you two decide together that you need help to work through the issue, get help. Find a good Christian counselor and make that first appointment. Whatever it takes, do it!

Dr. Kim: We have never dealt with infidelity but we know couples that have gone through this struggle. Has it ever been hard to trust me to be faithful to you?

Nancy: No.

Dr. Kim: It's the same for me. We both knew that that was somewhere we didn't want to go. I think we both knew we were vulnerable, but I think we knew, even when we were younger and stupid, to draw lines and not cross them or let someone else cross them.

Nancy: Yes, when I was younger I used to flirt. I was so young, but I knew in my heart of hearts it would never go anywhere.

Dr. Kim: Yes, I think so. I think girls want to know that they're attractive to guys and some of that probably goes with flirting.

Nancy: Well, when you're 20 years old it does.

Dr. Kim: What do you do that helps you to be faithful year after year?

Nancy: Well, it doesn't even enter my head anymore. When I was younger, I kept wondering what it would be like to be with somebody else, but I don't even go there anymore.

Dr. Kim: Yes, I agree. And I don't know that I ever really did. Obviously, I think other people are attractive, but then I would think about what we had and were building and it was not worth losing that. I think that conviction becomes stronger every year. And you get to a point where you think, and I've told people this, that if you work on the important things in your marriage and do what you need to do, it will get to the point where something outside of marriage is not attractive to you at all.

Nancy: Exactly.

Dr. Kim: I wouldn't want to go there. I don't want to do anything that would betray our trust that we've built together.

Nancy: Well, that and the fact that when we did break up, that one time, you really made an effort to try to repair the relationship. I think I sensed a real security knowing that I could always trust you, and that's one of the reasons I came back. Plus, we were best friends.

Dr. Kim: Yes, I agree and I think God played a role in that even when we really weren't pursuing Him then.

Nancy: True.

Dr. Kim: Even though we have not experienced infidelity, we have broken trust with each other in other ways. I think of when we first got married. We had accrued some credit card debt, and I didn't tell you about it. You found out and then I knew I had to be honest with you about everything from that time on. In my mind, I thought that not telling you was protecting you because I knew we were going to work it out. And we did, but it wasn't right to not tell you.

Nancy: Yes.

Dr. Kim: Do you think we had to rebuild trust then? How did that affect you?

Nancy: I think that we did. It affected me because I am so frugal and I never want to be in debt. It's a fear of mine, and I had trusted you in that area. And I think, even sometimes today, I'll question a few things about our finances, and maybe it goes back to that.

Dr. Kim: Yes, I think so, and you don't do it often but I know you're concerned about it. That's why I try to communicate well on finances. I think I do better now. A lot of it with our finances is that I've always really trusted God and He's been faithful to us—especially since we went into ministry, when we had no idea of what our finances were going to look like.

Nancy: Oh, He's been very faithful. But I think too that He's let us learn a few lessons and sometimes we have struggled. Not serious struggles, but we had a bad debt that we had to pay off.

Dr. Kim: Yes, absolutely. I think when we paid it off that probably helped you—because you asked me about it probably every hour until we paid it off. What does it take to rebuild trust in a marriage?

Nancy: It did, yes. Communication. I think you've just got to stay connected. Share your feelings with each other. Share the hurts, and the problems, and ways to deal with it, and then move on.

Dr. Kim: Yes, I think accountability is part of that and I always tell couples, if it's infidelity, that they need to find another person of the same sex to be accountable with. The spouse should not be the one who's asking you the questions about that.

Nancy: Oh, yes.

Dr. Kim: But I think in other things like our finances or things like that, it is being accountable to you. To let you know things and for you to be willing to let that trust rebuild.

Nancy: Yes.

Questions for You:
- Is there anything that keeps the two of you from trusting each other?
- What do you each need to do to either maintain or rebuild trust?

Acceptance

We all want to be accepted. On the grade school playground, I wanted to be seen as a really good athlete. When it came time to choose teams to play a game, I wanted to be the first one chosen. It made me feel accepted and validated my talents. But I was not always chosen first. Sometimes I was chosen last. That hurt. I felt neither accepted nor validated. Fortunately, there were a lot of recesses over the years and one day's defeat could be redeemed by the next day's victory.

What does acceptance mean in marriage? For me, it means that I can be totally and completely who I am and Nancy accepts me. Is it unconditional? No, because I can do or say things that even I cannot accept!

When I counsel singles who long for a future marriage, I urge them to always be themselves. They cannot try to become who they think the person they are dating wants them to be. Once someone goes down that path, they will feel that if they stop maintaining that image, the other person will leave the relationship. That is a really bad place to be.

I want Nancy to accept my thoughts, feelings, and actions. I want to be able to share everything with her. I want her to be able to look deep and see inside me and know that she will still love me. This too has been a process for us. I would share something that was vulnerable to me and see how she reacted. I think she did the same to me. If the other reacted in a good way, that encouraged us and we were willing to share more. We did not do this perfectly, but with God's help we were able to see the value in accepting each other. With God at the center of our marriage, we became each other's safe place.

In essence, for me it is seeking every day to be who God created me to be and for Nancy to embrace what God is doing. Do you want your spouse to try to change you into who they want you to be? Of course not. That is God's job.

Here is an interesting thought. Over all the years that we have been married, God has never done anything in either of us that was not good for our marriage. Let that soak in. If God is molding me and building things in me, none of those will ever be bad for our marriage. That is God's plan, and our role is to seek that and to rejoice in who God is molding us to be.

Dr. Kim: What does acceptance in our marriage mean to you?

Nancy: Well, actually it means a lot right now because I think that I've grown more accepting in the past year, even in the things that bug me and have bugged me about you. Nothing big, your little idiosyncrasies and things like that, but I really think that I've let go of those.

Dr. Kim: Yes, I see the difference. I know the pandemic affected us in some ways and made us look at things a little differently for a while. We obviously spent more time together during the first part of it, and I think because of where our marriage was, it was good for us.

But I agree, I think God's teaching us more about unconditional love. I don't think you ever completely get there in this life, but the goal is for me to love you just as you are, to not be critical of you.

If there's something that God tells me I need to speak into you, then I need to do that. But most of all, it's just letting you be who God created you to be because I know you seek Him and seek to be better every day.

Nancy: Mm-hmm, well, that goes back to growing up in a very critical environment. I still, until recently, held on to a few little things but I've learned to really let go of everything now.

Dr. Kim: Yes, I think your home had a critical environment. You know I love your parents but I think our households were so different and when we were in the early part of dating each other I would see some of the critical things in the household that you grew up in. It bothered me and I thought that had to affect you. And it did. And I think you being the oldest, you took on a lot of protecting your sisters, and you took the brunt of a lot of things.

Nancy: I did.

Dr. Kim: I know that affected you. So in our relationship, have you always felt accepted by me?

Nancy: Yes. And I will say that just this year I've really accepted the fact that you fully love me more than anybody else on this earth ever has or ever will, and just entering into that realization has made a really drastic impact in my life.

Dr. Kim: So what got you there?

Nancy: I think just letting go of some of the negative thoughts in my life about myself and negativity in general, and learning to see that you really do love me that much. For me, it is accepting how much Christ loves me first. Maybe that's what opened the door for me to really love you and know that's how much you love me. And it makes all the difference. It takes you into a deeper relationship.

Dr. Kim: I think it's interesting that you said that. We've been married 53 years and God's still doing things in our marriage that are good for us. It again amazes me how patient He is with us. I think He's taught me to love you pretty unconditionally and has for a long time. And maybe it was your background that kept you from fully embracing that.

Nancy: You're just a trusting, good guy. I was a bit of a twerp.

Dr. Kim: Well, thank you. I think a lot of it was that our families of origin were so different. That affected us both. If I look at my dad and my granddads, they were very kind men. So my models growing up were definitely kind, gentle men. I don't remember any of them raising their voice at me or their spouse.

Nancy: Yes, I remember that. But I think it's really just your genetics, plus being around people like that. Alcohol wasn't a problem in your home. So you grew up a lot healthier than I did.

Dr. Kim: Yes, and I don't think either one of us realized that at 20 years old. And God's taught us a lot.

What happens when we do not feel accepted by our spouse?

Nancy: For me that would be the times when I think you're a little critical of me. It really hurts. It makes me feel like crap.

Dr. Kim: Yes, because we all want to be accepted and loved by our spouse. And, yes, I think when you feel that way, it's probably situational and it doesn't last very long—for example, if we're playing pickleball and I get upset if you're not playing as well as I think you could play. I think I am doing better at that too. I try to speak into you more now and encourage you.

Nancy: Yes, you do.

Dr. Kim: I'm going to get a little bit off topic for a minute. I know our competitiveness has been an issue. We've tried board games, golf, tennis, and other things, and we just never were able to do that very well because we're so competitive. I think the fact that we enjoy playing pickleball together shows that we have made progress.

Nancy: Absolutely.

Dr. Kim: For us, acceptance has involved choosing our battles carefully. It is being more tolerant of each other. There are things that we fought about in the early years of our marriage that seemed important to us then but today our take on them has really changed. Our set of rules for each other has been recycled into a life of much more grace and acceptance. Fewer fights and more intimacy.

Questions for You:

- What does acceptance in marriage mean to you?
- Do you feel accepted by your spouse today?
- What do you need from your spouse in order to feel accepted by them?
- Have there been times in your marriage when accepting each other was a challenge?
- If consistently accepting your spouse builds intimacy, what first step can you take?

Empathy

While our kids were growing up, our lives, like most of yours, were very busy. They were always involved in a variety of activities and we wanted to be right in the middle of it. Even amongst all the activities, for the most part Nancy and I did a pretty good job of staying connected as a couple. Being a counselor and telling other people what they needed to do was a good source of accountability for me. How could I encourage people to do something that I was not doing?

Connecting is one thing, but having empathy for each other was another. For me, empathy is walking in someone else's shoes. It is trying to see things through their eyes, from their perspective. That was not always easy. It took time and deeper conversations than we were having most days.

Here's a great example. For years, I would come up with some great idea and share it with Nancy and then she would ask me questions about the idea. I felt she was throwing cold water on every idea I had. It was so frustrating. I was so frustrated. One day I was sharing this with a good friend and he brought up a very interesting observation. He said, "Maybe she is asking questions so she can understand your idea better and then support you in it." It sounded so simple when he said it. Of course that's what she was trying to do.

I was so thankful for this friend and the wisdom God gave him to help me see something that I was not seeing. Now when I share an idea with Nancy, I give her all the time she needs to ask questions, and once she has done that, almost every time she is completely on board. I just needed to look at things from her perspective, and when I did, it made a world of difference.

Nancy is very independent. It was one of the things that attracted me. Yet I could not just assume that she was okay all of the time. She married me to be her husband. She married me to walk through life side by side with her. To do that well, I had to learn what having empathy for my spouse was all about. It was not complicated. I needed to be intentional every day as I listened to her, observed her, and asked good questions. All of these helped me to see things as best I could from her perspective. It made a difference.

The more I have practiced, the better I have gotten and the more connected we are as a couple. Now, there are still times when I have no idea how to put myself in her shoes, but she appreciates the effort I am making and helps me understand what is going on with her.

When I do take the time to be empathetic, it is pretty awesome, and over the years it has brought us closer together.

Dr. Kim: How do we show empathy to each other?

Nancy: For me, it's when I know you're overworked and I try to make things better for you. It really hurts me to see you like that.

Dr. Kim: Yes, and you do such a good job. I think one thing we both have really been good at is trying to be intentional in showing empathy for each other. We're grateful for that and we share that. There have been some times in the last few months, because of our schedules and everything that's been going on in our lives, when I've really seen you show a lot of empathy at a time when I really needed that, and it really helped.

I always know you're on my team, but really it just made a difference. When you would protect me or say no to things because you felt like I needed rest, it meant a lot. Sometimes you surprised me by doing one of my usual chores around the house. It did mean a lot.

Is it ever difficult for you to be empathetic toward me?

Nancy: Well, sometimes I think you take it a little far. Like playing the "poor me" card.

Dr. Kim: What do you mean?

Nancy: Well, just saying things like, "Oh, my shoulder hurts." That kind of thing. You can be, kind of, sniffly about those kinds of things and it just makes me want to say, "Buck up."

Dr. Kim: And you do sometimes, right?

Nancy: Yes.

Dr. Kim: I was thinking, when we talked about family of origin, that may be where that comes from, because I got so much empathy from all my family members—especially my mom and her mother, who, oh my gosh, I could just act like some little thing was wrong and I got all of this attention.

I think the only time it's hard for me is when you do get angry. I guess when you get angry it frustrates me and it kind of makes me mad. And so I don't do my best at that time. Instead of saying, "Okay, why is she angry? Is she angry at me or is it something else?" I just get kind of, "Ah, I don't like that." And so I just am not empathetic and not as kind as I should be.

Does empathy strengthen our marriage?

Nancy: Well, of course.

Dr. Kim: Man, I think it's just taking the time to do it. But when I see things through your eyes or try to see things through your eyes, and ask God to help me, that helps me a lot. When I just say, "Okay, God, I don't get this. Help me see things through her eyes," and then He does, it is awesome. The more I understand you, the more I love you and the more I know how to love you better.

Nancy: Yes, definitely.

Questions for You:

- How do you show empathy for each other?
- When is it hard for you to show empathy?
- How does being empathetic with each other grow your marriage?

Nurturing and Growing Your Intimacy

We have looked at five types of intimacy and three things that I believe are essential for intimacy in your second half of marriage. Let's look now at ways to nurture and grow the intimacy in your marriage. For those of you who have kids at home, you will have more time once your kids leave. For others, your career might slow down at a certain point or you'll want to pump the brakes on some of your activities. Either way, it's likely that things will slow down and you'll have more time.

The question is, how will you fill or use that time? Do you use it to do all the things you now have time to do? Do you use it to really grow the intimacy in your marriage? Do you do a combination of these two, or something else entirely?

Most of us do not work on our marriage 24/7/365. Yet, if this season is to be what you want it to be, being intentional about your marriage has to be a priority. It is a unique season. Early in your marriage, you were trying to figure out marriage and life and how they best blended together. If you had kids, there were blessings but they probably created more challenges with finding time. When you had a demanding career and hobbies, your calendar was fuller. Now you are in a new season, or you can see it on the horizon. Now you have the time to take your marriage to a whole new level. How can you do that? Let's look at some opportunities.

Showing Gratitude

When did someone first teach you the importance of saying "thank you"? I can't remember exactly when but I always remember it being something that my parents expected me to do.

It wasn't like they were always reminding me to say it as a child, although they probably did. It was part of our family culture. My dad said "thank you" to my mom and she did the same to him. Whatever my parents did to develop that habit in me worked. I say "thank you" all the time. I say it to the checker at the grocery store, the barista at the coffee shop, the ticket taker at the movie, and just about everyone else that I come in contact with. I am really thankful that my parents made it such a priority.

You know what's interesting? Sometimes when I thank someone, they have a shocked look on their face. It's like they cannot believe someone took the time to say it to them. I share a lot about the mistakes we have made in our marriage, mistakes that have caused arguments, fights, and misunderstandings, but the thank-you thing we got right.

When we started dating, Nancy took it up a notch for me. She thanked me for things that no one had ever thanked me for before. When I opened and closed the car door for her, when I bought a meal or a movie ticket or anything else, and at the end of the date, she said, "Thank you." It was incredible and two things happened because of it: it made me more conscious of thanking her, and it made me want to do more for her.

Today, nothing has changed. I still hear the words "thank you" many times every day. In our marriage, these words have elevated the value of everything we do for each other. It keeps us from taking each other and the things we do for each other for granted. I know we have done this since our very first date but it never gets old. There have been times when I have taken it for granted, but today, for some reason, it means a lot. Maybe it is from seeing so many couples over the years that hardly ever used those two words toward each other. It just means a lot and I think the consistency of saying "thank you" helps build intimacy.

If we take this a step further, we run into gratitude. I think gratitude is "thank you" on steroids! Here are some examples. Like a lot of guys, I love to grill meat, and perfectly cooking a beef filet is my specialty. My dad was great at grilling. Since he owned grocery stores, steak was a staple at my home growing up. I wanted to carry on that tradition. When I grill the steak, Nancy not only says "thank you," but she usually takes it a step further by saying something like, "You cooked it perfectly again," or "I love the way you seasoned it." On a date night, she thanks me for the date and gets specific in telling me something she really enjoyed about the evening. All those thank-yous and gratitudes have never gotten old. They are a part of what we have built and are continuing to build in our marriage.

One more thing on gratitude that has an impact on our marriage. Practicing gratitude helps us focus more on the good things, the things we love, appreciate, and enjoy. It actually shapes our perspective! It's thanking God for my wife, and our marriage, and all He is doing to grow us closer to each other and to Him.

How are you doing with showing gratitude to your spouse? If this is not something you do on a regular basis, start today. Think of one thing to thank them for and then do it. Look for the opportunities that are there right in front of you every day.

Dr. Kim: You say "thank you" to me a bunch of times every day. Why?

Nancy: Why? Well, I'm polite.

Dr. Kim: You are and the more you say it the more I find myself saying it.

Nancy: Well, I do try to consciously think, *Wow, that's really neat that he's doing that*, and try to encourage you and thank you.

Dr. Kim: When I cook dinner, you thank me. Every little thing I do, you're very grateful. I think it has helped me do it better, and I think it has helped me do it more with other people that I find myself with. I think that example you set has really rubbed off on me. Not that I wasn't grateful; I just don't think I said it as much. I would think it but I wouldn't say it, and you seem to think it and say it.

Nancy: Well, the more I look around, the more I realize how blessed we are that we can even go out to eat. Many people can't do that. There are people who don't know where their next meal is coming from, so we should be thankful in all things.

Dr. Kim: Absolutely. How do I show gratitude to you?

Nancy: I think you live out your gratitude to me because you take care of me financially and emotionally. You're there for me. We've always been able to converse really well and I'm grateful for that. It brought us through a lot.

Dr. Kim: I agree; I think that was one of the strengths that we had. How has that made a difference in our marriage?

Nancy: I think we've become more grateful to each other and have an overall grateful attitude about where we are with our marriage, with our family, our health, just everything.

Dr. Kim: Yes, we talk about that and we are very grateful. I think it makes us aware of it and I think it makes us value what we have right now. And I think it has also helped us to be more generous with other people.

Nancy: Absolutely.

Dr. Kim: Coming out of COVID, I remember that when we'd pick up food, we'd tip as if we'd been inside for dinner, and we've just kept those kinds of things up—because we pick up food a lot and we just try to be generous without being showy about it. We both love being generous to people.

Nancy: Well, it's fun to be generous with somebody else, but it's fun to be generous in your own self. It is fun to be generous with you!

Questions for You:

- How do you show appreciation to each other?
- How could you do better at this?
- Rate yourself. Are you doing a good job, an okay job, or a not-so-good job?
- If this has not become a habit for you, begin working on it together today.

Being a Student of Your Spouse

This is absolutely one of the most fun things that I get to do in our marriage. It was born out of the idea that a lifetime is not long enough to learn everything there is to know about your spouse. Just think about it for a moment. We all grow. We learn new things. God builds new things into us. There is alway something new to learn.

After two years of dating, I thought I knew Nancy pretty well. We spent a lot of time together and talked more than I had ever talked to a girl. We were best friends. Sure, there is a lot of that 19-year-old Nancy still there, but if I had stopped studying her then, I would have missed so much. I watched her learn to be the wife God designed her to be. I watched her develop friendships and really care for other people. I saw the effort she put into being a mother and now a grandmother. I watched her grow spiritually and saw her consistently put God first. I could add a lot more, but my point is that we all change, and if we are not students of our spouse, we can lose connection. As a husband and a wife, we need to grow together and learn not only about each other but also from each other. Being a lifelong student of Nancy has helped me in doing that.

When Nancy was 26, her mother was diagnosed with cancer and given two years to live. She died ten years later. Nancy's mother was a strong and determined woman and cancer was not going to win the battle against her. She fought hard and actually did not die of cancer, rather a heart issue.

I was there when Nancy first learned of her mother's cancer. We went to Houston together for her surgery. Over the next ten years, I saw incredible strength in Nancy as she dealt with her mother's health issues. We had deep talks about faith and what happens when we die. She shared about things that I never would have known if I had not walked through this with her. I mentioned earlier how I was the one to tell Nancy her mother had died. I saw grief in her that day but I also saw her strength. Over the next few days, as we went to Houston to be with family and to attend the funeral service, I saw her handle her emotions in a way that was healing for her and at the same time being there for other family members. Nancy grew through that experience and I was there to learn from her and to support her. What if I had missed that experience? It shaped her in so many ways and I would not have had a clue what I had missed.

I was 12 when I knew that God was calling me into ministry. That came with excitement and then the fear of what it would mean. Over the next 23 years, I tried to shove that calling aside. I was bargaining with God. I told God I was going to be the best Christian businessman ever and serve Him that way. But each year the reality of God wanting me to do something different came back. I don't remember exactly when I first shared that with Nancy. It was probably after we were engaged. She watched me struggle with this year after year. Each year she would simply say, "I am with you, no matter what you need to do." That was great but it still did not get me where God wanted me to go.

Finally, at 35 I knew the battle was over. I knew I could not really run from God. Did I think I could hide from Him? I had to finally figure this out, and I needed Nancy to be there to walk through this with me. Some of our close friends agreed to keep our kids one evening. Nancy and I went to this little Mexican restaurant and sat in the back. For three hours she listened to me as I recounted every step of this journey. I was ready to submit to whatever God wanted but the problem was that I had no idea what that looked like.

That night she said two things that impacted the rest of my life and our life together. First she said that she was all in. It did not matter what happened; she was all in. She was by my side and would stay there. She knew the implications. I would be going back to school, then to seminary, and then maybe more school. I would be giving up a job that had provided well for us for these first years of our marriage. We had no idea how family and friends would react. Yet she was all in. If God was leading, she was following!

The second thing she said was that I needed to talk to a good friend of ours who was a Christian counselor. That week I called our friend and asked him to lunch. He was a great listener as I poured out my journey to him. Then he asked me one question: "Have you thought about becoming a Christian counselor?" I hadn't. I had never thought about it, but now I saw it as the final piece to this puzzle. It fit perfectly.

In my job, much of my time had been spent counseling employees. I was also working with a program helping young men who had been in jail for drug or alcohol problems. The purpose of the program was to get them headed in the right direction and to turn their lives around. The more thought I gave it, the more sense it made. I came home from that lunch and could not wait to tell Nancy the news. Within a month, I was enrolled in school and had been accepted into a Christian counselor training program and internship. Our lives changed overnight. I had no idea where the money was going to come from, as our income would drop 80 percent over the next two years. We did have some money saved but how we made it through those two years was truly a gift from God.

None of these changes were things Nancy had planned on or asked for, but Nancy was open to where God was taking us. She knew me, she trusted me, and she trusted God even more. She had been a student of me for 15 years. She saw things in me that I did not see. I know God works miracles but it is impossible for me to think that I would be doing what I am doing today without her full support.

There are so many benefits of being a student of your spouse, and in this second half of marriage, most of us have more time to do that. From both friends and patients in this stage of life, I hear comments like, "I just learned this about my spouse," "I love getting to know my spouse in ways that I had not discovered before," "This stage of life that I kind of dreaded may be the best season of our entire marriage." There is so much still to learn about that person who said "I do" to you many years ago. Don't let the distractions of life or the distractions you can create on your own distract you from daily being a student of your spouse.

Dr. Kim: What does "being a student of your spouse" mean to you?

Nancy: Over the years, I've studied you as a man, as a husband, and as a counselor. In all your different roles, I've watched you and learned what makes you tick. It shows me how to better relate to you, how to love you better.

Dr. Kim: For me, it's been fun because as God has changed you, He's changed me too. I love seeing and embracing the changes and trying to respond to you in a way that honors that.

Nancy: Oh, yes.

Dr. Kim: We've always prayed, but it's connected us on a deeper level now. When I saw that in you, it just encouraged me to continue to try to grow. I try to be more aware of what is going on in your life every day and how I can encourage you. How can I come alongside you? If you've had lunch with a friend, I want to know how it went. I want to give you a chance to talk about anything that went on.

Or if you're playing pickleball with friends, I always ask you how you did. I guess I always ask you if you won because I know you're competitive, so I figured that's part of a good answer or a good question.

Nancy: Sometimes it's not.

Dr. Kim: No, and you know what? I can tell, Nancy. I can tell by your response. If you say, "I didn't play well," your tone of voice changes and I think, *Okay, she probably needs a little extra love tonight because she didn't play well at pickleball.*

Nancy: We've got a rough life, don't we?

Dr. Kim: Yes, I know. Well, I think the other thing is your empathy; you have love for other people, for the downtrodden. I mean, you have such a heart for that. You volunteer with mobile meals now. You've volunteered in a soup kitchen and served meals. You've done a lot of things to try to help others. Then just watching you when you have a chance to interact with someone who is having a hard time or maybe you feel is a little downtrodden. You take the time to talk to them, spend time with them, get to know them, and you really do care.

If we're watching a movie, I always know who you're going to empathize with. It's going to be the one who's in the worst shape, the most downtrodden, or the one who thinks life's not treating them fairly or people aren't treating them fairly. So all of that helps me see your heart and how deeply you care. I think it helps just to know that and it helps me appreciate more of who you really are.

Nancy: Thank you.

Dr. Kim: You're welcome.

Dr. Kim: Has doing this helped our marriage?

Nancy: Oh, yes. How could it not?

Dr. Kim: I know. I think I studied you earlier in marriage but I looked at it negatively—"Oh, this bugs me" as opposed to being empathetic and asking, "What's going on and how do I come alongside her in that?" For me, it was immaturity and selfishness, and as God has helped me in those areas, it's been much better.

How do we do this in this season of our marriage? Do you think we do that differently today, in this season, than we did in the past?

Nancy: We've had many years to work on all this, to become more empathetic, and to fall more in love, and it just gets better. Time heals all things and time can work to a great advantage in marriage and in life. It's like they say, "Older people have more wisdom." I feel like I have more wisdom.

Dr. Kim: Well, you do, and I can see people coming to you for that and asking you things because you do have more wisdom. But I think just being older doesn't make you have more wisdom. I think it comes from pursuing God. I think it's learning to persevere through things instead of pushing back on them. There are things in marriage we've learned to go, "Okay, we've got a problem. We've got to work through that." I think all those contribute. I don't think you get to be 60 years old and suddenly you have all this wisdom.

It's a constant process and I think it's the same thing with our marriage. It is constantly investing in it, working through hard things, learning from those, and seeing how each one of those steps grows us closer to each other.

Nancy: It pays off.

Questions for You:

- What is one thing that you have learned about your spouse in the past month?
- What can you do as a couple to make sure you are students of each other?
- What is one thing you have learned by being a student of your spouse that has made a positive difference in your marriage?

If you need some help in this area, take the Awesome Marriage 18 Day Wife Study Challenge and the 18 Day Husband Study Challenge. You can find it at AwesomeMarriage.com under Resources.

Focus

Have you ever been reading your Bible and when you finished you had no idea what you just read? Have you ever sat in church and completely lost focus on the message your pastor was preaching? Have you ever had the deer-in-the-headlights look at your spouse when they finish talking to you because you heard absolutely nothing that they said?

If you answered yes to one or all of these, welcome to the club. Know you are far from alone. We are all wired differently. We think differently. We may lose focus for a myriad of reasons but the bottom line is the same for all of us. Losing focus is not good for our relationships. Let's flip the script for a minute. What if you are the one talking and your spouse is the one who loses focus? Now how do you feel? You have just shared something really important to you and your spouse did not hear a word of what you said. None of these help our connection, and depending on the situation and the state of your marriage at the time, they can disconnect us.

Nancy and I both can struggle with this. We are thinking about something else and have no idea what the other said. I get frustrated and she gets hurt. Neither of these grow our marriage. So what can we do? First, we need to be aware that we do have a choice. So we need to make the choice that favors our spouse. If Nancy is talking to me—especially when it is something important to her—I have to face her. I need to be looking in her eyes. I need to eliminate distractions. That means that my phone is put away or on silent and I'm not looking at it. It means that my focus is on her words, her tone of voice, and her body language. I want to understand all that she is saying. I want to be able to respond to her in a way that lets her know either that I really heard what she said or that I was really trying to understand and need her to help me get there. We hear all the time that love is a choice, and it is, but so is focus. Look at it this way: if you are focusing on your spouse and they know you are focusing on them, won't that make a difference for both of you?

One thing that helps me focus is that Nancy and I have routines throughout our day of "distraction free zones." Every day when I get home, Nancy and I spend 5 to 15 minutes catching up. We try to not let our phones interfere with our time together, and that has made a big, positive difference for us.

Recently, I asked Nancy about an obligation that was on our calendar that I didn't know much about. She did a great job of letting me know what the event was all about, why we were invited, and why she thought it would be good for us to go. Despite all her effort, I heard nothing. I was distracted. When I realized I had mentally left the conversation, she had finished. I didn't want her to know that I had not really been listening. I waited a minute and then asked her a question about it. Guess what? My question had already been answered. I was caught. We worked the situation out but it was clear how important it is to focus on our spouse, both for us and for them. The effects of not focusing are huge and the benefits of focus are enormous. I have a choice. You have a choice.

I think that when we have the potential for more time together, it is easy to fall into this pattern of not really focusing on your spouse. In this season of life, not focusing on your spouse is a huge temptation. The proximity we have to our spouse and the time we have with our spouse can lead us to falsely believe what they are saying is not important or they can tell us again later. Fight this temptation! Focus on your spouse and listen well when they are speaking. How are you doing with focus on your spouse? Don't answer yet—first, ask your spouse how you are doing.

Dr. Kim: How do you know if I am focusing on you or not when you are talking to me?

Nancy: If you don't answer my questions. Or you'll be somewhere else entirely and you'll say, "Now, what'd you say?"

Dr. Kim: Yes, I've done that. I used to think I could multitask. I'm coming more and more to believe you can't multitask and do both things well.

Nancy: Well, you can't listen for sure if you're multitasking.

Dr. Kim: I was guilty of that, especially in busy times. I wouldn't just get on my computer or look at something on my phone; it would be in my mind. So I could be sitting there with you and you thought I was listening, and then if you asked me a question, it was like, "Oh, crud, she asked me a question. What in the world did she say?"

Nancy: Yes, I can daydream too.

Dr. Kim: We both can do that but I usually know when you are; if you're looking at something, or doing a crossword puzzle, or something like that, I know that's your focus. I've learned, unless it's an emergency, to let you have that time and then I can talk about it later. I was getting to where I'd forget some of those things—probably because they were not that important anyway. Now I just write them down and when you get time, then I talk to you about it.

How do you feel when you realize I have not heard a word you've said?

Nancy: Angry.

Dr. Kim: How does it come out?

Nancy: I usually let you know verbally.

Dr. Kim: Like, "You're not listening to me," or something like that. It's frustrating when we don't listen to each other. I think part of it is that we listen so well to each other most of the time; so when we don't, it's just like, "What are you doing?"

Nancy: That's why we try to have time every day where it's just you and me. Nothing else. No distractions.

Dr. Kim: Absolutely. What helps you focus?

Nancy: I realize that I need to keep things out of the way and really seek the one thing that I'm trying to do or to say. I try not to let my mind wander, which it tends to want to do.

Dr. Kim: Yes, I feel that I do much better, like we're doing right now. When I can look you in the eyes and we're talking, my mind doesn't wander. I think we have trouble when we really are not looking each other in the eye. So it's easy to be focused on what's in front of us instead of the other person.

Nancy: Or thinking about something else I want to say to you. If I'm holding a thought until you finish, then I don't hear whatever else you've said.

Dr. Kim: So what do you do when that happens? Or what could you do differently?

Nancy: Well, obviously I need to realize that if I needed to talk to you about that one point that it's going to come back to me no matter what. So then I just listen.

Dr. Kim: Yes, I think it's easy to do that, especially if I have a point I want to make and you're still talking. If I keep focusing on that point, I'll miss what you're saying. Then when I give my point, you don't hear me because I ignored what you said. So I'm trying to do a better job than that.

Questions for You:

- How well do you focus as a couple when the other is talking?
- What distracts you the most?
- How do you feel when you know that your spouse really heard you?

- Are there specific times in the day or routines you can make where you can put away all distractions and just talk to and focus on each other?

Time

Quality time or quantity of time: If you asked me which was the most important of these two in a marriage, I would say both! That's not a cop-out. It's what I really believe. They are both essential.

If you have a limited amount of quality time to spend together, you enjoy it and leave wanting more or feeling shortchanged. If you have all kinds of time together but there is no quality to the time, you may even think you wasted your time. None of us gets this right all the time. There are a lot of contributing factors, but trying to make the time you have together quality goes a long way in continuing to grow your marriage. If you only have 15 minutes together, you can either make them the 15 most quality minutes possible, or you can just blow it off thinking 15 minutes is not enough time to connect.

Since Nancy's love language is quality time, I have learned a lot about it over the years. I know that just sitting in the same room with her watching TV usually does not count as quality time. If we are sitting close together in the same room, and I am interacting with her about what we are watching and also rubbing her back, then it counts!

We all need to set aside time to really be with each other. A friend of mine and his wife both retired a few years ago. They sleep in the same bed and then wake up and go their separate ways the entire day. They regroup for dinner, watch some TV together, and go to bed, usually at different times. They have more time than they have had in their entire marriage to spend time together but they do not. Recently I asked my friend how retirement was going. He listed off all the things he does now, and not one of them included his wife. That broke my heart to hear because he is missing out on quality time with his wife. Don't be that couple! Make time for each other and pay attention to the quantity of time and the quality of that time.

Whether you are still working or retired, you have time. Don't think that as you get more time the two of you will just naturally have more quality time together. You have to first make it a priority and then you have to make it happen.

Dr. Kim: What is your favorite quality time with me?

Nancy: Well, the pinnacle is being able to go to the beach with you and take a few days away, but I love our times together every day, where we just take about 30 minutes to talk about the day, what's happening in our lives or in the world.

Dr. Kim: I agree. It's when we have time without distractions. I think that's why we love the beach so much. We don't go to the beach to do 90,000 things; we go to the beach to be together, lie on the beach, talk, spend time together, enjoy God's creation—those kinds of things. I think that's why it's our favorite quality time for both of us. I love it. I also look forward to coming home to you in the evening. If I'm working at home, then it's when I quit working and we come together for the evening.

Nancy: Yes, I do too.

Dr. Kim: What happens to us when we do not make time for each other?

Nancy: I was thinking about this the other day. I think if we let it go too long, it's like a little wedge between us and we have to pull that wedge away and start communicating again.

Dr. Kim: I do too. It just seems like after knowing you for almost 55 years that I have more stored up but you don't. Your tank empties pretty quickly. It's one of those things in the way God made us that we've got to keep filling that up.

Nancy: Exactly.

Dr. Kim: I think that taking out time every day, which we've done so consistently for so long, has helped a lot. I remember after Grant was born, it wasn't long before you were just saying, "We need our date nights again." Because being a new mom and being with the baby all the time I think you needed something to look forward to. And you knew that on date night we wouldn't be interrupted and we could be together. So we started having a weekly date night pretty early.

Nancy: Yes, we did.

Dr. Kim: So we could be connected and I think both of us looked forward to that. We knew we were going to have that kind of quality time.

Nancy: Mm-hmm.

Dr. Kim: How do you make it a priority?

Nancy: Well, I look forward to it! So I'm going to do what I look forward to. I can't imagine what I would do if I didn't look forward to it. There are a lot of couples that do not do that well. I'm thinking of a couple that we know. He's just not a good communicator; he doesn't want to talk. I encourage her to try to sit down and sit with him for a little bit, to see if that'll open him up. So far that has not worked for them.

Dr. Kim: Well, you both have to want to. If it's just one of you, it will not work. A couple in that situation can get some help. I want people to see the value in that time together. I think if you do it consistently, you'll see a difference in your marriage. You'll see you're closer together, you're more intimate, connected with each other, and your marriage is better.

Nancy: Exactly. You know, that brings up another thing: mentors. So many people say, "Well, we can't afford counseling." If that's the case, find a godly couple that's been around the sugar bowl looking for the handle longer than you and just let them guide you, help you, spend time with you, and mentor you. Ask them to show you which way to head. Everybody needs that.

Dr. Kim: There is help out there. If you're in a church, ask your pastor; ask your small-group leaders. Find somebody older than you who will share with you.

I think as guys, it's good to find another guy a few years ahead of you who seems to have a good marriage. Ask him if he can spend some time with you. Be completely honest. Say, "I don't know how to communicate. What do you do?" Then let him just share some things with you and let God use that.

The other thing is prayer. I think sometimes as men, we don't value that because we don't know what to do, so we put it off. But if we really pray that God will help us communicate on a level with our spouse that we both need, God will help us do that.

Nancy: I also think a good Bible study is so helpful for men and women, getting in the Word, sitting under different teachers who are teaching the truth. You start learning about God and His Word and how much He loves you. It's going to make all the difference in every relationship, especially in your marriage. I can't think of anything that I find more valuable, for my life and my marriage, than the time I've spent in Bible studies, and I still do.

Dr. Kim: The fact that we've grown and shared our faith together has been so good for us. It has given us things to talk about. If you're seeking God together and you're in Bible studies and you're reading the Bible together, that in itself is going to give you things to communicate about.

Nancy: Right. And it's good to have community with other believers. But there really is something incredibly important in the fact that you get into a good Bible study and stay there for a while, or forever.

Dr. Kim: And see what God does. Well, it's been life changing for you.

Nancy: Absolutely. The more you know about Him, the better your life's going to be. And everybody I know who has tried it says the same thing.

Dr. Kim: Yes. When you really started getting into Bible studies was the time I went into seminary. So I was studying and learning things in seminary. You were studying and learning things in Bible Study Fellowship.

Nancy: Which I highly recommend; it's international.

Dr. Kim: I just remember that we would share things and learn and grow, and I learned from you and you learned from me. In fact, we've even done one of the Women's Bible studies together. I didn't tell any of the guys, but we did, and I learned a lot.

Questions for You:

- How much time are you spending together regularly? Is it enough?

- Think about the amount of *quality* time you have together now. Is it enough?
- Define for each other what quality time means to you.
- What can you do to improve the quality time you spend together?

Final Thoughts on Intimacy

At the beginning of this section, I shared about the difference between intimacy and sex because I think it is important to separate them, and our culture does not do that well at all. Intimacy covers so much more of our marriage that the sex act. As we have looked at emotional intimacy, intellectual intimacy, physical intimacy (nonsexual), experiential intimacy, and spiritual intimacy, I hope that has opened your eyes to the various kinds of intimacy that are in a healthy marriage.

In looking at the essentials of intimacy, we looked at trust, acceptance, and empathy, and how important they are in continuing to build your marriage. Finally, we looked at the importance of being grateful to your spouse, being a student of your spouse, focusing on your spouse, and having good quality time with them. The intimacy in a marriage is such a crucial part of what makes marriage the close, connected relationship we want it to be. It also overflows into the sexual relationship. The three sections of this book are in this order for a reason. If you get love right and if you get intimacy right, then sex almost takes care of itself. Our tendency is often to jump to the sex section first, but building the foundation of love and intimacy will only make your sex life better.

Part Three

Sex

We all hope for great sex in our marriage relationship. For many couples sex starts out as a home run. Not to say that it's perfect, but it often starts off exciting and fun. The attraction you have for one another, and the hormones that go along with it, both go a long way in early married sex. But over time life gets complicated. Work, kids, and all kinds of things take our time and energy. Far too often, sex gets put on the back burner. It's not like the flame has gone out. The fire is still burning, but it's set on simmer instead of on high.

Then there are our expectations about sex. Going into marriage, we can have high expectations that sex will bring us a lot of fulfillment. We see sex portrayed in books, magazines, movies, TV, streaming, and on every single media platform there is! It dominates the covers of many magazines and unfolds in the pages of books. There are self-proclaimed experts who seem to have it all together in this area and offer their words of "wisdom."

With all of this, we may expect that a good sexual relationship in marriage will be a slam dunk. But it's not. Couples struggle. They can struggle early in marriage and later in marriage. When we struggle, most of us have no idea how to get things back on the right track, let alone build something. I believe God's plan for sex was designed for marriage. I believe it can be great for a lifetime. Sex is a gift from God. He is the one who created the sexual relationship. He is the one who made our bodies in such a way that they fit perfectly together.

A good sex life is like everything else in a good marriage: it takes work. It takes communication. It takes time and effort—both at the beginning of a marriage and in every other stage a marriage goes through.

Looking back, at 20 and 22 years old, Nancy and I had so much to learn—about each other, about life, and about sex. I want to share with you a few of the things that we learned.

- We both thought about sex. I just thought about it a lot more.
- I learned that making her feel guilty so she would have sex worked in the short term but was very damaging in the long haul.
- Before we had kids, we had a lot of time for sex; after we had kids, we had to be really intentional to make sex happen.
- A lock on our bedroom door was one of the best investments that I ever made.
- Our sex drives were different. That was not bad but we had to learn how to navigate that.
- We learned what we liked and did not like in sex.
- I had wider boundaries when thinking about things to do in sex and I had to stay at her comfort level.
- In certain seasons of life, we had to be very intentional or sex did not happen.
- We discovered that learning about each other and sex was going to be a lifelong project.

What if we asked God what He wants for you in your sex life in your marriage? What do you think He would say? Would He say something different today than He would have when you began your marriage?

Here are some of my thoughts. Sex was designed to knit a couple closer together. It was designed to give both spouses pleasure. Sex helps protect us from temptation. Sex brings the physical, mental, emotional, and spiritual all together for a couple. God designed sex for us to enjoy.

In the Old Testament book Song of Solomon, Solomon talks about enjoying his wife's body, how both he and his wife are fulfilled, the closeness the sexual relationship brings them, how it helps to grow their love for each other, and how their commitment to each other deepens through sex. In one chapter, Solomon starts at the top and works his way down his wife's body. In another, he starts at her feet and works his way up her body. He writes of enjoying making love to his wife all night long. His wife cherishes the way he loves her and cares for her. She willingly gives herself to him. That is what God intended. That is what God has for you.

If I asked you what you wanted your sex life in marriage to look like in this season of marriage, what would you say? Would you both say the same thing?

With everything in life, you have to know two things: what you want, and how to get there. Otherwise, you're not going to get there. To start, you have to define what it is you want. Then you have to figure out next steps on how to get there.

If I get in my car and say I am going to Washington, DC, but don't have a map, GPS directions on my phone or car, or an app that can direct me, will I get to DC if I just start driving? Maybe, but the odds favor no. Even if I do, it will take me longer than it should have and I will have experienced a whole lot of frustration along the way. The same is true with your sex life. The two of you need a map to help you get where you want to go.

Dr. Kim: Is sex different for us today than it was in past seasons of our marriage?

Nancy: Duh.

Dr. Kim: Boy, what do you mean by that?

Nancy: Well, of course, it's different. We've gone from lust to love. It was all physical; everything was physical.

Dr. Kim: Yes, we were 20 years old. It was physical. But it did connect us, don't you think?

Nancy: Well, yes.

Dr. Kim: But, yes, it was definitely passion, and hormones, and all that kind of stuff. So how do you think it's changed over the years?

Nancy: Well, it's about the physical, of course, but there's also the spiritual—just becoming one with the one God created you for; and it's just what God created. It's beautiful. It's good.

Dr. Kim: I think, for a guy, the visual part of it probably hasn't changed. I'm as attracted to you today as I was back then, and I think that's important for a guy. I love the closeness that it brings us, and there is that spiritual component that a Christian couple can have.

We really feel connected, that God gave us this gift and we're embracing it together. Matt Chandler calls it "the mingling of souls." And I think that's a good description of it. It's not just our bodies connected. It's our minds, our emotions, and everything's connected together.

Nancy: Well, you called it *dod*.

Dr. Kim: Yes. It's the Hebrew word for "the mingling of souls."

Nancy: There you go. That happens now for us and did not really happen back then. But I want to go back to something you said, that you're still attracted to me. A lot of men are not attracted to their wives, and a lot of wives are not attracted to their husbands, and I think that can be a real issue as you grow older. If you haven't grown together spiritually, that can be a real problem.

Dr. Kim: I agree, yes. I've known couples that have changed. I think it was Pastor Tommy Nelson who said, "You look your best on your wedding day and after that it's all downhill." That's kind of true in some ways. I think what I've seen in some couples is that they've been through things, or maybe had surgeries or something, or are just aging, and when they go through those things, and they are connected, and they value their marriage, and they've worked on it, they are still attracted to each other. There's an attraction there.

Nancy: But the key is if you've worked on your marriage and you've grown together. And I think an important facet of that is growing together spiritually.

Dr. Kim: Yes, I agree. I think that is the thing that makes the difference. We see stories of couples much older than us, or married a lot longer than us, and you can just tell that they adore each other. They are connected. And they wouldn't want anything else but each other. And I think we are growing into that.

Nancy: Right.

Dr. Kim: I think it's fun how God created it. When we were younger and our hormones were going crazy, there was a lot of lust. That was a part of that season of our marriage. It is what God gave us and it was awesome. Then as we were raising kids, life began to take on some deeper meaning. I think that begins to give you opportunities for your sex life to take on deeper meaning, as long as you're working on it and are focused on it.

Nancy: So what if somebody comes to you and says, "I'm just not attracted to her anymore," or "I'm just not attracted to him"?

Dr. Kim: I ask them, why is that? Then I help them figure it out. In other words, have there been some fights? Have there been things said that have been hurtful? Those things can affect attractiveness. I've had couples that looked like they could have stepped out of *People* magazine, yet they didn't have any attraction for each other because of what had gone on in their marriage.

So the physical part of it attracts us in the first place. When I first saw you, I was attracted. I wanted to know more about you. So you have to have that attraction to start with.

I think for those who nurture their marriage, that attraction is always there because you see more in that person than just the outside. You don't see aging; you don't see other things like that because you are past them. If you haven't grown your marriage, then I think it's easy for that attraction to go away.

Nancy: So what does somebody do at that point? How do they go back and find it?

Dr. Kim: In counseling, once we identify the issue or issues, we can begin to work through them. Ultimately the goal is forgiveness. Hopefully, with both spouses there, we can then begin working on healing. Prayer is part of the process—prayer for healing and for God to restore the sexual attraction for each other, and to not only restore it, but to give it back to them or give it to them in a way that would deepen their love for each other.

Then we begin rebuilding the marriage. We find out what their love languages are and talk about how they can meet each other's love language. We talk about how they can be kind to each other. We explore how they talk to each other. When those things are in place, it changes the way you look at the other person. So I think it's going to be a process. It's not like they come in for a session and, *BOOM!*, everything is okay. It is a process of healing and believing the truth that you can be attracted to your spouse all your life.

Nancy: Well, that was going to be my next question, because I know of a couple who are a couple of years older than us and they would say that their sex life was part of their past. And that's so sad. I mean, if you're physically able to have sexual intercourse, then I think you should do that forever—and not just give up on it.

Dr. Kim: I agree. I think that if you're physically able—and some people aren't and we will talk about that later—then it needs to be a priority. Maybe that is what people did before we had some medical help, like ED medications and things like that. One couple I counseled, it's been a few years now, but they were in their early 80s and it was a second marriage for both of them. Both had lost their spouses a few years before and now found each other and were going to be married. They wanted to talk about their sex life because they knew how important it was in their marriages before. Both had long, healthy marriages and they wanted sex to be a part of this new marriage.

I think that if a couple told me that they they were content without sex and asked my opinion, I would tell them, "I think you're missing out. If you're physically able, then I think you're missing out."

I was talking to a lady recently, and because of some physical things, she's not able to have sex. So we talked about the other things that they can do. So now there's a lot of holding, cuddling, and everything but intercourse really. She said that she misses the sex that they had but she said, "I think we're still very close and intimate in that way and it draws us together." And so I think that even if there's some reason you can't have intercourse, there are still a lot of other things that you can do to be intimate with each other and to care for each other.

Nancy: Right. Because I know that it's still a big part of our life, and when we don't prioritize it, I feel that we grow a little bit apart.

Dr. Kim: Oh, I think it definitely connects us.

Nancy: I do too.

Dr. Kim: I think you're right; it's what we talked about in the intimacy section on communication. We have to have that every day. Not that we have to have sex every day. I mean, it would definitely be okay with me, but it has to be a regular part of our life. And I think it affects us both.

Nancy: Right. I would like to see people embrace the fact that it is a big part of marriage. That is the way God designed it to be and He wants you to be able to enjoy that for as long as you can.

Dr. Kim: It is a gift. It is a gift that God gave us. Some people think God is a prude. God is not a prude. God created our bodies to fit perfectly together. He did all this. He wanted us to have this. He created orgasms. He created all those things, like our skin receptors that fire up when we're close to each other and when we're intimate with each other. If it's something that a couple struggles with, I would want them to do everything they can to make it good again.

Nancy: Right. God created it for us.

Dr. Kim: Sometimes, as guys, maybe we're embarrassed to talk to a doctor or a urologist about ED, but I think we have to get past that.

Nancy: Gosh, it's on the radio all the time.

Dr. Kim: No kidding. Almost every other commercial on Sports Talk radio.

Nancy: I guess it's pretty common.

Dr. Kim: I think it is common or there wouldn't be 5,000 different places you can go to get help.

Nancy: I can remember when we were at a conference once where you were speaking and a woman came up to me and said her husband had prostate cancer and had a treatment, and he didn't want to have sex anymore and she was crushed. I asked her if they had tried medication and she said he wouldn't even do that. So that's a case where they need to seek professional help individually and together.

Dr. Kim: Yes, and probably some counseling together to see why he has given up on sex. Maybe he has a fear of not being able to keep an erection or something like that, but you don't know until you try, and then you can go back to a urologist and say, "Hey, this worked," or "It didn't work."

I hope that we're healthy enough that sex continues to be a part of our marriage for the next 50 years.

What has our sex life done for our marriage?

Nancy: Well, I think it has enriched it in a huge way. It connects us in a way that nothing else can.

Dr. Kim: Yes, and you know this because I tell you, but I look at you and just am in awe of you a lot of times. I'm just so attracted to you and I think our sex life being good over the course of our marriage is a part of that.

Nancy: Well, it hasn't always been good; there have been ups and downs. We had to really try to rejuvenate that part of our marriage at different times. But we both wanted to and we did what we needed to do to get there.

Dr. Kim: Would you say that the times when we did struggle with it were probably some of the most difficult times in our marriage?

Nancy: Yes.

Dr. Kim: Because we'd set sex aside for a while and then it went on for a long period of time. We needed that connection to pull us back together.

Nancy: We did. And I was amazed, when we finally did get back together sexually, how deeply it made me grow in my love for you.

Dr. Kim: That's cool. And that's a good point. So even when you go through these hard times, if you come back together, God is going to bless that. That's what sex was created to do. One of the purposes besides pleasure is to help us grow closer to each other.

Nancy: Absolutely. I asked my gynecologist once why women sometimes don't want to have sex, because most men do. And she said, "Women are like a box with all these drawers. You open this drawer to make sure your hair looks okay. Does he look attractive? Are the kids in bed?" There are so many different things that go around in our minds to have sex. We just need to keep it simple.

Dr. Kim: Well, and I think I've said it a lot of times, a woman's greatest sex organ is her mind. That's why I think as a woman, and you can answer that, you have to focus on it.

Nancy: That is so true. Absolutely, you do. Because even as you age, you're not thinking about it as much as when you were younger.

Dr. Kim: I think guys, most of us, think about it a lot more than our wives do. But we don't have a box with a bunch of drawers in it. I think we just have the box.

Nancy: One big drawer. And it's open all the time.

Dr. Kim: I think it's just that we have to understand each other. We have to realize we don't think about sex the same. But we both need to focus on it so we can have what God wants us to have.

Question for You:

- What do you want most out of your sexual relationship in your marriage in this stage of life?

Talking About Sex

Learning to talk about sex together in a way that strengthens and enhances your sex life in your marriage is one of the best things that you can do for your marriage. Maybe you have done this well throughout your marriage, and maybe you have not. In the counseling room, I have very rarely talked to couples who have. But it is never too late, and since you are in this season now, it is the perfect place to begin. Let's look at three areas that are essential to talk about.

First, frequency. It's essential that the two of you get on the same page with frequency. Doing so removes one of the biggest hurdles couples face when seeking a healthy sex life. We have to talk about frequency. But what we want is to talk about it, not argue about it. This means you each communicate how often you'd like to have sex, listen to one another, then come to an agreement together. It may require compromise. I'll give you helpful guidelines to work through below.

Second, what do you like and not like when it comes to sex? You have to define this in order to define the goal. If you were to make your checklist of what goes into quality sex for you, what would be on your list? In marriage, we need to know these things about our spouse. We need to talk about them. It helps us focus on what works and stay away from what does not work.

Third, what gets in the way of having the sexual relationship you both want now? What are the hurdles you need to face, deal with, and overcome together? The hurdles in your marriage need to be talked about so you can develop a game plan together to deal with them.

Many couples avoid the sex conversation because it has turned into a fight in the past. They don't want to risk having it happen again. But it doesn't have to be that way! Our goal is for you to have a productive conversation for your sex life to be better for both of you today and to lay the foundation for the rest of your marriage. Don't lose sight of that.

Here is a suggestion for how to have this conversation:

- Sit facing each other.
- Don't interrupt each other.
- Really listen when the other person is talking. Listen to understand, not to answer.
- Be able to say back to them in your own words what they said. This shows you understood what they said.
- Don't try to solve everything or talk about everything at one time.

- Remember that anything your spouse says is not a criticism of you; it's feedback you both need to hear to reach the goal together.
- Don't take what your spouse says personally. You don't know what you don't know. Your spouse is not grading you, because there is no test. You are simply working on a common goal together. So anything they say is not a knock on you; it's just information that will help you two work together to obtain the goal.
- See yourselves as a team working together to solve a problem.
- The goal is a win for each of you and for your marriage.

Frequency: What's Normal?

People ask me all the time what "normal" is regarding frequency. This is my answer: Don't ask what's "normal" in general, rather ask, "What is our normal?"

Asking how often married couples have sex can be a dangerous question because the answer is what works for that couple in this season of life, and it may be very different for each couple. "Normal" is a moving target. You can define your normal for today but that may change in five years.

So when you begin to talk about frequency, don't start with "what is a normal sex life?" Start by defining your normal in this season. That is really the only thing that matters. Comparison can really get us in trouble here. Every couple is unique, therefore what works for them as far as frequency is unique to them and their lives together.

Let's define your normal: Marriages are different, lives are different, sex drives are different, and schedules are different. You want to take all that into consideration when deciding your normal. What is realistic? Whether you have sex once a week, twice a week, every day, twice a month, or once a month, does that work for you both? When we fight over frequency, our focus shifts and we are no longer embracing the gift of sex in marriage as God intended. Your sex life will never be great until you quit arguing over frequency.

But don't miss this point: frequency is not the issue. The issue is how you handle the frequency issue together. As you talk about it, the goal is not to convince your spouse to see things your way. The goal is to really listen to each other and find a middle ground and a balance that works for each of you. Remember, you are not setting your normal for the rest of your marriage, only for where you are today.

In my experience working with couples, agreeing on expectations about frequency really helps your sex life. Neither of you wants to be rejected, but oftentimes the spouse with the higher sex drive gets rejected a lot. This starts a negative cycle that can really damage your sex life.

If you have an agreed-upon expectation about frequency, it's much less likely that the spouse with the higher sex drive will get rejected as often. For example, if I want to have sex five times a week and Nancy wants to have sex two times a week but we don't have an agreed-upon frequency, I might ask for sex every day. That would frustrate Nancy and I would end up getting rejected a lot. I'd likely feel frustrated and quit asking after getting denied two times in a row, and then we'd be in a slump where sex was nonexistent.

Instead, let's say that we've agreed to have sex two to three times a week. We've talked about it, heard each other out, worked to meet each other's needs, and met in the middle. Now that I know the frequency is going to be around two or three times a week, I'm not going to ask for sex every day. I know sex every day is off the table. Instead, I'll initiate a reasonable number of times in a week based on our sex conversations and what we've agreed to. Nancy isn't going to say no very often because I'm not asking too much. She feels respected because I honor our agreed-upon expectations and understand that every time I initiate I won't get a yes. Both our needs are being met and we both feel respected. We both know what to expect. We can still be spontaneous and have a little "extra sex" when the week is right. The best part? We are connecting via sex two to three times a week and our connection deepens as we have fun in the bedroom.

Stick with the frequency conversation until you reach a solution that works for both of you. So be willing to compromise. Once you agree, try it for a month and then talk about it again. Is it working for you? If not, what needs to change? Think about it this way: If you are not fighting over frequency, what could that do for your sex life?

Dr. Kim: How has our frequency changed over the years?

Nancy: Well, there've been highs and lows but that doesn't necessarily have anything to do with age. I would say we're as active as we want to be right now. I think you've got to be on the same page, obviously.

Dr. Kim: Yes. I think it's something you've got to talk about. In this season of life, what is our frequency? What do we want? What do we both want?

Nancy: What's right for us?

Dr. Kim: I think, for us, it's that we don't have to worry about somebody walking through the bedroom door anymore because nobody's here but us. So we've got a lot more flexibility, which helps, for sure, because you don't have to worry about other things. That probably helps you.

Nancy: Yes.

Dr. Kim: I know that when our kids were little, you worried about them. Were they okay? Moms want to be able to hear their baby. Then as they get older and you lock the door and you know they are out there, it's a little harder for a woman to focus. So now it's a lot easier.

Nancy: Right. Well, that's why we often encourage people to just get away for a night or so or put the kids at Grandma's or at the neighbors, or somewhere where you know they are safe, and just have a romantic evening at home for just the two of you.

Dr. Kim: Yes, because sometimes we need that jump start.

Nancy: Yes. I think that's what makes sex in this part of our lives even more attractive, because we have so much freedom.

Dr. Kim: Yes, I agree. Except for the times when we struggled with sex because of other things going on in our lives, our frequency probably has not changed that much over the years. It really has been, other than the first year or something. Since the first year or so of our marriage, we've kind of settled into a norm in our sex relationship that works well for us. But everybody's different.

Nancy: I agree. I remember recently you said that you're amazed at the way men and women in counseling talk much more freely about sex than they used to. So if that's an indication, maybe it means that people are talking about sex more.

Dr. Kim: Oh, I think so and I think it's so good. I can remember in my early years of counseling couples, I'd want to talk about sex with them because I knew it was an issue in their marriage. It was awkward to bring it up. Now it's pretty normal that we talk about it.

Nancy: Yes.

Dr. Kim: I feel much freer to ask somebody, "Okay, how's that part of your relationship?" People are much more open to talking about that. I think a lot of people are trying to figure out God's plan for sex, as opposed to what the world tells us. The more they want to know about God's plan for sex, the more they begin to see that this is how sex was created to be. You don't need anything more today than Adam and Eve had in the Garden of Eden: their two bodies. They didn't need anything else, and I'm guessing their sex was good. They were naked all the time.

Nancy: Well, they multiplied.

Dr. Kim: What obstacles have we had to work through?

Nancy: We've already talked about having young kids. We've had periods of bouts with depression or illness or something that took away from our sexual intimacy.

Dr. Kim: Obviously, after you had your hysterectomy, there was a period of time when we couldn't, but we were still very intimate during that time. Then when I had prostate surgery, 15 years ago, there was a period of time when my body was adjusting. It was important to both of us for our sex life to come back. We had good doctors who helped us.

Nancy: Right.

Dr. Kim: It's always been something that we knew was important for us. We were going to do everything we could, whatever the obstacle was, to overcome it. I know there will be some people who are reading this who are going to say that they have obstacles they haven't been able to overcome, and I get that. That goes back to what we talked about earlier, finding other ways to be very intimate and close with each other.

What do we want it to look like today?

Nancy: I think I want more of the same and to continue to pursue the spiritual part of sex.

Dr. Kim: One other thing I was thinking about is that today we are very relaxed in our sexual relationship. There's no tension. It's really relaxed, and enjoyable, and just very good.

Nancy: Yes.

Questions for You:

- What is your frequency now?
- Does that work for both of you?
- What frequency will work the best for both of you?

When Does It Happen?

However you answered the frequency questions, now comes the issue of making "normal" happen. When does it happen? Where does it happen? Are there any obstacles? Should sex be spontaneous or scheduled?

If Nancy and I decide that for the season we are in sex twice a week is to be our normal, then we need to talk about when or where. Otherwise, a week may pass with no sex, which could be frustrating for both of us, especially after all the work we put in to get to this point. For example, if we decide on two times a week, does that mean once during the week and once on the weekend? Or both times on the weekend? Morning or evening? Or some other plan? Is it all to be spontaneous, or do we need to do some planning?

Many of us cringe at the idea of scheduling, because in our mind sex is supposed to be spontaneous. We definitely felt that way at one point in our marriage, but that was before kids! So we decided if scheduling helps, why not schedule it? It really helped.

We schedule other fun things and other important things. You schedule vacations, date nights, trips, potentially life-saving doctors' appointments, big projects that matter to you, and so much more. So why not schedule sex? Does scheduling a vacation make the vacation less exciting? Certainly not! Scheduling sex doesn't have to make sex less exciting either.

For us, in certain seasons of our marriage, scheduling sex gave us something to look forward to and I think it really helped Nancy get her mind focused on those days. I have never needed the help to get my mind focused. That never seems to be a problem!

Here's a little counsel on this for you. Deciding on two times a week does not limit you to two times a week. Two is your normal frequency, but if the two of you agree on more, go for it. If one of you is sick, do you still have sex twice that week? Maybe not. There are always exceptions. Just don't let the exceptions become a new normal that undoes your hard work on this.

The whole purpose of talking about frequency is to help you get into a rhythm with your sex life that you both enjoy and that happens as you planned, draws you closer to each other, and grows your love.

Let's switch from quantity to quality. If you are having sex every day but there is no quality to it, what have you accomplished? Even more, what have you missed out on? Let's look at quality.

First, when we talk about quality sex, how do we define quality? Here's my definition: quality means that both spouses enjoy the experience. The key here is knowing what the word "enjoy" means to each of you.

Does it mean that we both have an orgasm every time? No, not necessarily. If we define successful sex only by reaching orgasm, I think we can run the risk of missing out on some great sexual experiences, as well as putting unnecessary pressure on ourselves and our sex. But let's talk about this. My experience as a husband and a marriage counselor is that if one doesn't have an orgasm, it's usually the woman. Now, does not having an orgasm mean the sex was bad? I think too many people think that it does and I think that puts their sex life in a box. Even if a woman doesn't have an orgasm every time, it does not mean that she does not enjoy the experience: it still feels good; she may love the closeness, attention and intimacy. As a guy, we want to please our wives; but, guys, you have not failed if your wife does not have an orgasm.

So listen up: that is not the gauge. Don't miss the experience because you bought into that idea. Communicate. What makes sex quality for her? Ask her. If orgasm is important to your spouse each time, then work on that together. Ask her what she needs you to do. What helps her? Work on her having an orgasm first. But if she says she is okay if she does not have an orgasm every time, trust her. It is okay. You have not failed.

Dr. Kim: How would you define quality sex?

Nancy: It is when we are really able to take the time to spend together, work to make sure each other is pleasured, and then sense that spiritual aspect of it.

Dr. Kim: Yes, for me, obviously, orgasm is important. I don't know if I can describe it, but there's just a closeness that is there that I love, and I love it when we have time to spend afterward with each other. I love that part of it, when we're able to lie there together afterward. We may talk, we may not talk, but we are very close together.

Nancy: Yes.

Dr. Kim: I think that would be a lot of the quality for me and I like what you said too. It's fun when we can have a nice romantic dinner or something like that. Those times are great but it doesn't always have to be that. I don't know if that affects the quality. I think it just sets the atmosphere. I think it makes it easier for a woman to get her mind focused on sex, if you're in a romantic setting, for sure.

Is having an orgasm every time important to you?

Nancy: No. I enjoy the closeness and making sure that you're getting exactly what you need. That gives me pleasure right there.

Dr. Kim: I think that for many years in our marriage you always had an orgasm. Then for whatever reason, it hasn't become as big a priority to you. But I had to adjust to that, that you were still getting pleasure and you were still enjoying sex, even though you didn't always have an orgasm.

I think part of the criteria that I had in my mind for sex was that I wanted to please you. I had to help you have an orgasm every time, and so it was an adjustment I had to get used to. I needed to know that was okay with you and that wasn't something that you felt like you had to have every time and it really wasn't causing you to look at sex in a negative way—that you did see more to it than just having an orgasm.

Questions for You:

- How do you each define quality sex?
- Is having an orgasm every time important to both of you?
- Depending on how you answered that last question, what would help?

Embracing the Differences

Making the effort to understand your spouse is essential when talking about sex. We are different, and not just in our anatomies. Most of us have figured out by now that there are differences that we may not totally understand, but accepting them makes a huge difference in our sex life. Like any topic we are diligent to learn more about, our study of male and female differences will help the conversation about sex move forward.

I helped write and teach a "learning about sex" class for fifth and sixth graders. The boys and girls were taught separately. It was so interesting that most of the boys' questions centered on the anatomy and how things worked physically. On the other hand, the girls' questions centered on the relationship. It does not change as we get older. Men tend to care more about the sex act. Women tend to care more about the state of the relationship. That is not an absolute, and sometimes the roles are reversed, but here I am speaking about the majority. Here's an example for you. There have been times in our marriage when I looked at Nancy and thought she was the sexiest thing I had ever seen, but at the same time, she looked at me and thought of how impatient I had been with her that morning. There is so much value in this difference though; we learn from each other. We each learn to value what the other wants. We learn to communicate our needs and desires, to work together, to keep short accounts, and how important sex is in our relationship. Our sexual relationship is always better when our overall relationship is better. When we both embrace these differences, our sex life is so much better.

Here are a few other differences that are important for us to embrace. Most men have more frequent desires and needs than their spouse does. I think the fact that men are very visual plays a big part in this. Most men have wider boundaries in sex. In other words, what we think about concerning sex can be different from what our wife is thinking about. This is not a right or wrong thing, just a difference. Women on the other hand tend to place more value on trust and commitment. They need to feel safe. They also want to know that their husband enjoys the time that he spends with her. What we do not want to do is let these differences become obstacles. We need to embrace them.

Dr. Kim: What differences have affected us?

Nancy: I think the visual part is different. Visual doesn't really help me very much.

Dr. Kim: I know, and I look so good.

Nancy: That's true.

Dr. Kim: I think sometimes a woman cannot imagine that her husband is thinking about sex because she, like you said, has all the "drawers" to deal with. I don't have my hair fixed. I don't have my makeup on, and on and on. Yet sometimes, and I've told you this, I've thought you were the sexiest when you thought you looked your worst.

You could look sweaty and I think, *Gosh, she looks hot.* Or you could have your hair up in a towel after washing it and you've got mascara streaming down your face and you walk out of the bathroom and I'm thinking, *Wow, she's so cute.* Sometimes I think you look at me and wonder, *What is wrong with you?*

Nancy: Yes, I have, but I love it at the same time. It's nice to know that I'm attractive to you and that you want to be with me.

Dr. Kim: Yes, that's good to know.

Nancy: Yes, keep it up.

Dr. Kim: Are there any other differences we have not mentioned? I definitely think that when the kids were at home, it was difficult for you to not think about them or what they were doing when we were having sex. Today we don't have to deal with that anymore.

Nancy: Right.

Questions for You:

- What differences are affecting your sex life?
- How can you begin to embrace these differences?

Bonding and Other Fun Stuff

There is one more area that I don't think we talk about enough. Over the two years that Nancy and I dated before we married, there were a lot of ways we bonded. We held hands, I put my arm around her shoulders, I put my arm around her waist, we looked into each other's eyes, we cuddled, and we kissed.

Once we were married, we didn't focus as much on those. The act of sex moved to the forefront, which is normal for a lot of couples. What we realized after that, though, was that we missed the nonsexual bonding. All of those little things brought about the enjoyment and closeness that grew our relationship and attraction in the first place. So we began to make an effort to build those back into our marriage. These ways of bonding are important and we do not want to let them slip away.

Have you let the nonsexual touching slip away? Share with each other what kinds of nonsexual bonding you most miss or enjoy most, then commit to get those going in your marriage: more conversations, hugs, holding hands, an arm around the other's shoulder, cuddling.

Dr. Kim: So what is your favorite way of bonding with me?

Nancy: Actually, it's conversation.

Dr. Kim: Nothing physical?

Nancy: Well, there are certain things that I really like. For example, when you come home and you kiss on my neck, I enjoy that. And when you tickle my back, things like that. But usually I get most of my jollies from just talking to you.

Dr. Kim: Yes, which, as a guy, is like, "Wow. That is amazing." My favorite way of bonding with you is probably cuddling. I love cuddling in bed before we go to sleep. We sleep very close together and so we're cuddling in one way or another most of the night. I like that.

Nancy: Yes, me too. You're warmer. You are my personal heater.

Dr. Kim: Yes, and you're always cold. At the end of the day, when I turn out the light by my bed, you're usually still reading, but I love just getting close to you. I like that this day is done and I am cuddling with my favorite person in the world.

Nancy: Yes, it's special.

Dr. Kim: Yes, it's very special.

Question for You:

- What is your favorite type of nonsexual bonding?

Romance

Romance is important. Some guys really get this. My dad did, and as a result I do a pretty good job most of the time. My mother's love language was gifts. Her love for gifts began in her childhood, since her dad often gave her little gifts. It was a way he showed love to my mother and my grandmother. When my parents married, no one knew about "the Five Love Languages," but my dad figured it out and the gifts he gave to my mother made her feel loved.

He did well at other things too. The way he respected her and spoke to her showed his love. He took her on dates and trips and loved spending time with her. I wanted Nancy to feel loved and tried to do a lot of romantic things for her. I loved the way she responded and she was so thankful for everything I did.

Most couples I talk to say that the romance before marriage was good. The problem for many guys is that after they get her to say yes, they set the romance aside. It served its purpose and they think they and the marriage can exist without it. We stop being intentional with romance, think that it no longer matters, or just get lazy. We may have ideas but never follow through on them. You may think you can live without romance, but can your wife? If the romance in your marriage has slowed or is nonexistent, it is time to rekindle it.

A good place to begin is with your wife's love language. Since Nancy's is quality time, anything I do that gives her quality time with me is seen as romantic. Giving her my undivided attention without any distractions is romantic to her. It is not so much the restaurant or beach or adventure. It is the quality time.

Recently Nancy had a minor surgery. She needed my help a couple times a day changing the bandages. I found the perfect bandage on Amazon and ordered a box of them. Then two times a day, I helped clean the incision, apply the medication, and then bandage it. This went on for three weeks. One day after I had finished with the bandage, she looked at me and said, "I am so in love with you." That time and attention were romantic to her.

I share that to help the guys see that the opportunities to be romantic come in a variety of ways. You may think that you cannot be a Romeo, but I guarantee you are married to a Juliet. If you are still stuck, here are some suggestions: Do what you did before marriage. If it worked then, it will probably still work now. Find out what says "romance" to her. Just ask her. After all, she is the expert on her! Google it. Ask Siri or Alexa. You have no excuse!

A lifetime of awesome sex happens when we take action. When we talk about frequency and quality and differences in sex, we need to take action steps. Sex in marriage seems to come in cycles. Each cycle becomes an opportunity to talk about this season you are in and what each of you needs to do—individually and together. If the romance has died down in your marriage, today is a great day to rekindle the flame.

Dr. Kim: What is the most romantic thing we have each done in our marriage?

Nancy: I think it was one of those times, in the early '90s, when the kids were still home. We had just been in a dry spell, maritally, sexually, in every way, and we went to the beach and it just was an amazing time. It was magical.

Dr. Kim: It was pretty magical. From the moment we walked into that hotel room, music was playing. It was just a romantic setting.

Nancy: It was so nice.

Dr. Kim: It was so relaxing. We walked out onto this balcony, and there was the Caribbean ocean in front of us, which is so beautiful. I think we would both say that was probably more romantic than our honeymoon.

Nancy: Oh, by far, yes.

Dr. Kim: Yes, and maybe what we had learned about each other over the years made a difference too.

Nancy: Honeymoons are overrated.

Dr. Kim: Yes. I don't know what we expected going into that trip. It was our twenty-fifth anniversary. We didn't plan that trip to jump-start our sex life, so I think we were both surprised at what happened on that trip.

Nancy: Right.

Dr. Kim: That was the trip when you picked out a cologne for me that you really liked. I still wear it hoping that it will still have the same effect that it did then. And it does sometimes. It was just a real magical time for us, and I want couples to experience that. That's why we talk to couples about planning and having a getaway if they can. You don't have to spend a lot of money. You could go to a bed and breakfast or something similar. The point is just to get away together. And I think on our honeymoon, at 20 years old, there were a lot of unspoken and unrealistic expectations on my part. In my mind I had a quota of how many times we were supposed to have sex on our honeymoon. I think the honeymoon was fun overall, but it didn't even compare to what we experienced on our twenty-fifth anniversary trip.

Nancy: Right.

Dr. Kim: For me, the most romantic thing would be some of the romantic evenings that we've had at home—when we have dinner together with candlelight, and talk, and then make love. It is just special. I love those times.

Questions for You:

- What does romance mean to each of you?
- Share your most romantic time together with each other.
- What do you want romance to look like today?

Making Sex Better

We've set the stage for talking about sex and making it happen. When it does happen, you want it to be satisfying for both. Three things to help get there are sexiness (hold on, I'll explain) and two types of foreplay. (I'll explain that too!) I don't want you to miss out on how these can boost enjoyment in your sex life.

Sex is everywhere and it is easy to buy into the world's view of what's sexy. In your marriage, it does not matter what the world thinks is sexy. It matters what the two of you think is sexy. It's not about lingerie, silk boxers, or anything like that; it's about taking care with our appearance. This communicates that your spouse is worth your effort and energy, even after all the time you've been together.

When Nancy and I were in college and had a date, I wanted to look my best. I actually thought about what I wore. I showered, washed my car, and wore cologne (which she picked out). I wanted to make a great impression. Most of us want to when we're dating. But once we are married, the "best impression" gets replaced by seeing each other first thing in the morning and late at night, at our best and at our worst. In marriage it's easy to fall away from making an effort since we know we're in a secure, committed relationship. But our spouse deserves some effort and intentionality from us.

For the guys, take care of yourself. Remember how you used to get ready for a date. The small things matter: fresh breath, boxers that aren't full of holes, a shirt you know she loves to see you in, a put-together outfit, and making sure you smell nice. Continuing to make the effort to clean up and care for our hygiene, clothing, and appearance can go a long way. Much like romance, it shows you are thinking of her and want to keep pursuing her. So don't neglect this. It will make her feel very special.

For the ladies, honestly, you do this much better than the guys do. I realized a long time ago that all Nancy really needed to do to be sexy was to keep breathing! My guess is that will work for you too. However, I do hear from a lot of men that they appreciate when their wife makes an effort to look her best for him. In my experience, for men it's not that their wives are literally more attractive when they make an effort, but that it shows they really care about us when they make the effort to put on a nice dress and throw on some lipstick. When you make an effort to look nice, it tells your husband, "Hey, I want to look hot and it's all for you—just you."

A lot of foreplay happens outside of the bedroom. Connecting through good conversation, shared activities, fun and laughter forms the bond that leads to sex. It's 24/7/365 foreplay, which is basically how you treat each other the other 23+ hours of the day, and it can make a huge difference in the bedroom. How does that work? Consistently put your spouse's needs in front of yours. Know what your spouse's needs are. Ask your spouse daily how you can help them today and what would make their life easier or better today. Speak to each other with gentleness, kindness, and respect. Apologize when you fall short of that standard. Take time out of your day to text an "I love you" to your spouse. Plan a date for the two of you. Foreplay done consistently day after day will improve both your marriage and your sex life.

Then once you're headed into the bedroom, don't just skip straight to the sex act. Have some fun with foreplay. Take showers or baths together, give your spouse a back rub, kiss, give massages or foot rubs, snuggle together naked, or just spend some intimate time together. Foreplay may not happen every time, but commit to working on improving this part of your sex life. What does your spouse like best? What gets you both in the mood? In this season, most of us have more time for foreplay, so take advantage of that time.

Dr. Kim: What is foreplay to you?

Nancy: Talking.

Dr. Kim: I love that you said that because I think our sex is best when we are connected outside of the bedroom.

Nancy: Exactly.

Dr. Kim: When we've just had fun together and we've communicated well, we feel this closeness, and that carries over to the sexual relationship. For you, it's really the ways that we connect outside the bedroom that contribute to a good sex life.

Nancy: Yes. There are times when we get in bed and you're like *BOOM!* and I'm like, "Where did that come from?"

Dr. Kim: I wonder at times about that too! Yet it's when we're both on the same page with it that makes it really romantic.

How do we make an effort to remain sexy to each other?

Nancy: Well, I try to look my best all the time for you. I don't like it when I don't look good when you come home, or when you leave. I just want to look good for you.

Dr. Kim: You do. I love that. I appreciate that. I don't think it's a requirement that I put on you though.

Nancy: No, not at all.

Dr. Kim: I love you just like you are. I think that's been something that's important to you though. I think we've both tried to remain healthy. We can't always control what our bodies do or don't do in a lot of ways, but we can try to be as healthy as possible. It's not about trying to look sexy for each other: it's about being healthy for each other, which helps in having a long life together. Taking care of yourself is really important.

Nancy: And you just enjoy life more.

Dr. Kim: Yes, absolutely. You've always had this look that you give me that is very sexy.

Nancy: Really?

Dr. Kim: Yes, you just look at me in a certain way with your eyes. Your eyes are so expressive and you'll look at me like that and I think, *I can't wait until we get in bed.*

Nancy: Oh, wow.

Dr. Kim: And sometimes it's going to be a long time before we get in bed and I think, *What am I going to do for the next two hours while we're at this party?* Also, I try to make you laugh. Sometimes the things I do or say make you laugh and at other times they don't.

Nancy: No, sometimes it's the eye-roller.

Dr. Kim: As a guy, we always want a formula. I do something that makes you laugh or excites you one time, and then I do it the next time and you look at me like, "What are you doing?" I guess that's the way God created us. There's no formula.

Nancy: No.

Dr. Kim: When do we do the best at 24/7/365 foreplay? I would say it's when we're consistent with the things that we know make our marriage better. So, for me, when I get unselfish and I think more like I'm supposed to and put God first and you next, then I'm doing a better job as a husband. I look for things to do to help you, ways to have fun with you, to make you laugh, all those kinds of things. For me, 24/7/365 foreplay is just making the effort by knowing you and what's going to make you feel loved, and cared for, and to help you out.

Nancy: I'm almost always trying to do that.

Dr. Kim: So what do you do?

Nancy: Well, I try to make myself look attractive to you, and I try to do things for you, and just to anticipate something that you might want or need.

Dr. Kim: Yes, and when you cook one of my favorite meals, I love that. Because you don't have to. We're at a point now where we do pick up food a lot because there's two of us. There are some meals we really enjoy that we have to fix at home because they're special, and nobody cooks them the way you do.

Questions for You:

- What is your favorite form of foreplay?
- How do you define sexy?
- How can you implement 24/7/365 foreplay into your marriage?

Obstacles

Let's talk about the hurdles or obstacles that get in the way. Our first hurdle was one many couples face: having children. After five years of marriage we were ready for our family to grow. We loved having a baby in our lives and embraced the changes that came with it, but sex became a challenge. I'd ask Nancy at bedtime if she wanted to have sex. She'd say yes and then she'd fall asleep before I could get my clothes off! The energy that we had both always had for sex was often difficult to find.

I was frustrated, and she hated that I was frustrated, but we were in a totally new season of marriage. The key for me was to realize that this was a season and it would not last forever. When I accepted that fact, it made a real difference. We talked about adjustments that we needed to make together. Our frequency changed, but once we talked about it, our quality didn't suffer. It was about dealing with expectations and making them realistic for that season of marriage. We learned to talk more, plan more, and embrace the changes. We were more aware of opportunities that we needed to take advantage of, like the kids' nap times, overnights with grandparents, showers in the morning.

Over the years there have been other obstacles that came with different seasons. Our schedules could get out of whack and leave little time for us. We had to learn to be intentional with our schedules, how to say no, and how to schedule time for one another. We have dealt with health issues like surgeries, cancer, and a heart attack, which all affected our sex life for a while.

Lower libido is an issue for many couples. Then the reality is that things like depression and anxiety can have a negative effect on sex. The key for us in each season we have been through was taking the time to listen and to understand each other. We had to talk about the obstacles and not ignore them. We had to listen, be empathetic, and be nonjudgmental. We had to go through these together as a team. When we did that, our sex life during and on the other side of these obstacles was better and our marriage grew.

Dr. Kim: Do we have obstacles in our sex life today?

Nancy: Getting busy and not focusing. Not doing the things that I want to do to make for a more enjoyable time. I get wrapped up in other things, hobbies, work, or different things like that. I then realize that I haven't taken that time to focus on you.

Dr. Kim: It's interesting you say that because both of us still work and many other couples in our stage of life don't. It's not right or wrong; it's just different. I think what we experience is because we're very busy, but even couples that are retired and have more time can still get too busy to focus on it. Just because you have more time doesn't make it happen. You still have to be intentional.

Nancy: Exactly. Somebody can be busy even if they're not leaving the house.

Dr. Kim: Yes, and not think about the other person or their sex life. The other obstacle I think about can be if we have something physically wrong with us. When I broke my wrist would be an example. I've had rotator cuff issues and have had both shoulders operated on. Those are some physical things that we've had to go through, but we've overcome.

Nancy: Sure.

Dr. Kim: We had to learn how to adjust our sex life during those times. We tried out different positions that worked because we couldn't do it in a position we were used to. So being flexible and being willing to try something different have been important for us.

Nancy: Yes, we don't really have a great many obstacles.

Dr. Kim: No, and I think we haven't done a lot of negative things to complicate our sex life.

Nancy: Like what?

Dr. Kim: Well, an affair or something like that. We don't have things like that to deal with.

Nancy: Oh, yes. We haven't had any time in our marriage where we've been unfaithful to one another.

Dr. Kim: I think that maybe we should say a little bit about that. Some people do have obstacles because of the past, maybe infidelity, maybe pornography. I would say it's never too late to deal with those. Maybe get counseling so you can come to a place of forgiveness and reconciliation. God can heal that and God can give you something at this stage of life that's more fulfilling than you could ever imagine. If you take that step, God will be there for you.

Nancy: Right. Well, you've seen it happen in your practice.

Dr. Kim: I have. And I've seen it happen with all ages of people.

Nancy: Exactly, and there are so many good things out there now to help people. Other than counseling, there are mentor programs, books, and all kinds of things.

Dr. Kim: Yes, and recovery groups like Celebrate Recovery. There are a lot of ways to help people get back on track. It's just, again, being willing to put the work in and knowing that it will be worth it.

Questions for You:

- What obstacles do you see affecting your sex life today?
- How can you best deal with these?

What Do We Really Want?

Recently, Awesome Marriage surveyed a group of married men and women. The group consisted of a variety of couples, with responses from newlyweds all the way to couples that had been married over 50 years. With that wide range of marriage longevity, the age range of these couples also varied greatly. Some were in the first and some in the second half of marriage. We asked them to list the five things that they wanted from their spouse in the sexual relationship. It was interesting to see that the responses across the age groups were very similar. The circumstances varied but the things they wanted in sex did not. As we look at the responses, I want to see how each of them play out in the second half of marriage.

If I asked you to list five things that your spouse wants from you in sex, what would you put on your list? Would that be different today than in the first part of your marriage?

As we go through marriage together, we learn about each other in almost every aspect of life, including sex. Yet, if we do not talk about our sex life with each other, we can get into a sexual rut. I firmly believe that this season of marriage can literally be the best sexually. Why? Many of the distractions are gone and most of you will not have kids living with you anymore—at least not full time. You have the freedom to develop your sexual relationship into something very special for the two of you, but you have to talk about it. I hope that some of you have a great sex life now. If that's you, be grateful! But like anything else in marriage, if it is going to stay good, you have to keep working on it. Some of you are struggling with your sex life or have become complacent about it. Some of you have packed it away somewhere in the attic!

I believe that God gave the gift of sex not just for when our hormones are raging or to have a family. It is a gift that can be enjoyed for the lifetime of your marriage. I also believe you would have skipped this section if sex was not important to you. So let's begin by looking at this list of what I think couples want out of sex in their marriage. I want you to have the tools to understand each other better and to be the best lover you can be.

Sex is not about you. It's about the two of you. Nancy and I married young, and as far as sex, we grew up together. At 22, I believed way too many of the myths surrounding sex—myths like, women always have the same sex drive as men do, and women get turned on in the same ways men do. In truth, many women have a strong sex drive, but in most marriages the husband's drive is higher than the wife's, especially in the area of frequency. Men are visual. It takes very little visually to get a man going. There are times a wife thinks she looks like a mess and her husband is thinking she is the sexiest thing that he has ever seen. And for men, our wives want us to look nice and to smell nice for them but the visual turn-on is just different.

Men and women are different and usually think differently and value different things. We communicate in different ways. These differences can affect our relationship with each other, especially if we don't take the time and exert the effort to understand each other. Differences can draw us together or push us apart, and they can improve or wreck our sex life in marriage. Many couples spend their whole marriage fighting the differences in each other instead of embracing them. You will never have the marriage or the sex life that you want in your marriage if you do not try to accept, understand, and embrace each other's differences.

A husband and a wife are a team, and if your marriage is going to succeed, it takes both of you working together. I think Nancy and I did pretty well at the team concept over the years of our marriage, especially after we took divorce off the table. Being a team is essential.

Dr. Kim: What do we want in our sex life in our marriage in this season?

Nancy: More of the same: security, trust, time together, and to continue growing spiritually. I really enjoy our times in the evening when we watch the Bible Project or read a devotional together. That is something I really cherish.

Dr. Kim: Yes, and I think all that goes into feeling closer to each other.

Nancy: Absolutely.

Dr. Kim: I don't know where I first heard this but believe it is true: couples who regularly pray together have a better sex life.

Nancy: I agree.

Dr. Kim: Because a woman loves to have her husband be the spiritual leader and to engage in that with her. When they do, it draws them closer together.

Nancy: Absolutely. Women want their husbands to be godly. They want them to be strong leaders, even in this age where women are strong and independent and all that. It's still wonderful to have a husband who is the leader. You walk side by side together but let him be the leader.

Dr. Kim: I would reiterate what you said. Obviously, the physical part of it is very important to me and I love that and I look forward to that. So I would want that to always be there. I love the fact that we're enjoying our sex life and still trying new things.

Nancy: Yes.

Questions for You:

- What do you want in your sex life in your marriage in this season?
- How can these best be met?

What Husbands Said They Want from Their Wives

1. A Husband Wants His Wife to Be Engaged

Remember, you are a team. It seems that many times women think that their husband could and/or would have sex with them whether they are engaged or not. As a guy, that can be true at times, but those are not the times that we husbands hope for. A husband does not want a body to perform on. He wants his wife to be engaged.

What exactly does that mean? Look at it this way. A man's greatest pleasure in the sexual relationship is pleasing his wife. Let that soak in. In so many ways it is countercultural, but in talking to husbands for over 35 years, I have seen that it is absolutely true. Your husband's greatest pleasure in sex is in pleasing you. The focus in sex is on the two of you together. He wants you to enjoy sex with him. He wants to please you. He wants you to express your love for him. He wants to have fun with you and to be playful.

Let me explain it this way. Ladies, you know how good it makes you feel when the two of you communicate well? How you feel when you know your husband gets you and what you said? It draws you closer to him and increases your love for him. Guess what? Sex is his communication; it's one way he wants to communicate with you. Being engaged is not just for him. It is for you too. When you are fully engaged, I promise your enjoyment will increase, and that is a win for your team.

In the early years of our marriage, sex was different than it is today. The hormones we had at 20 were different from those we have today. In those early years, we had Song of Solomon sex. Solomon delights in his wife's body. He caresses her breasts. He makes love with her all night long. The "all night long" may be gone at this stage of life—or maybe not—but enjoying each other can still be there. Sure, none of us look like we did on our honeymoon, but honestly, that does not matter. The spark can still be there.

Pastor Tommy Nelson says that we look our very best on our wedding day and it is all downhill from there. Whether that is really true or not, he makes a good point. The ways we change over the years do not have to affect our sex life negatively. I saw it in my grandparents and in my parents, and my belief is that they enjoyed each other sexually their entire lives. So, ladies, if you are passive in sex, why not work on being engaged? Tell your spouse what he can do to help you. Every person can be sexy at any stage of marriage. Wives, you can embrace your sexiness today and I guarantee your husband will love you for it.

Here are some practical ways to be more engaged in sex:

- Let your husband know when you are enjoying sex. This might mean verbally telling him during sex, moaning or making noises, or showing him with your facial expression that you are enjoying it.
- Try new lingerie or a special perfume. These kinds of gestures tell your husband, "I'm ready for sex and want to do this with you."
- Initiate a kiss or a specific position or sexual act with your husband. Initiating tells your husband, "I'm here."
- Most importantly, try to truly be engaged mentally in the bedroom. It's so easy to get distracted. But if you feel your mind wandering, narrow back in and really concentrate on enjoying the moment with your husband. Focus on your body and his body and what you are doing.

Dr. Kim: Is it ever hard for you to be engaged in sex?

Nancy: Yes, if I am not in the mood or if my mind is somewhere else.

Dr. Kim: So what do you do in those situations?

Nancy: Well, if I know that it's something that you really want at that time, I just adjust my mind to try to meet that need for you.

Dr. Kim: Do you feel comfortable saying, "Can we do this later?"

Nancy: Oh, absolutely and I do that some. Sometimes I'm just like, "No way, I'm just not there right now."

Dr. Kim: Yes. But you don't say that out loud. I think I've heard you say, "Can we do this later? Can we do this tonight? Can we do this in the morning?" Or something like that.

What helps you be engaged?

Nancy: For me, it's pre-thinking and pre-determining. If I know we're going out for the evening, or we're staying in, or whatever it is, I just decide that I'll stay engaged.

Dr. Kim: Yes, that's good.

Questions for You:

- Husbands: What does having your wife engaged in sex mean to you?
- Husbands: How would you practically like to see your wife engaged in sex?
- Wives: What can your husband do to help you engage?
- Wives: How can you plan to intentionally be engaged with your husband in sex?

2. A Husband Wants His Wife to Be Open

In other words, be willing to try new and different things. Most couples are pretty good at this in the early part of their marriage. Then I think we can lose our motivation. We fell into this in the years that our kids were at home. There was a lot of "hurry up" sex. After our kids went off to college, we stayed in this hurry-up pattern for a while until one day we looked at each other and said, "We do not have to hurry!" So we made a date to talk about our sex life and what we wanted it to look like.

I could think of things for us to try sexually that would never have been on her radar and I did not expect every idea that I threw out to fly. The win for me was that she listened to me and I listened to her and if we were both not on board, we took that idea off the table. She was open and yet knew she could say no. It was information I needed. Plus, there are so many things we can do in our sex life, it was not going to suffer when we took something off the table.

Husbands, I have to get real with you here. It's so important that you stay at your wife's comfort level. It's important to always stay at the comfort level of the spouse who is least comfortable. If she says no, respect her no. Don't lose trust and respect with your wife by pushing her. And it's important to note that a pouty husband is a pushy husband. If you pout when she says no, then you're not really respecting her no. Your sex life will thrive with mutual love and respect. So respect her boundaries and respect when she says no to things.

I encourage you to talk openly about what you want, be open to new ideas, be honest with each other, and respect what gets taken off the table. I am fully confident that with mutual love and respect, you can have an awesome sex life with what the two of you left on the table.

Today our sex life is great. It is great for this second half of marriage. What we had in the first half of our marriage was great for that season. We have probably three positions that we both enjoy. We have more time for foreplay and we take advantage of that. We rub each other's backs. We take showers together. We caress each other. We talk about our sex life and continue to work on making it better. I think we both listen to each other better than we used to.

Here's where we are going to get completely real about the "second half" part of this book (hey, you decided to read it!). In this season there are some positions that just are not comfortable for one or both of us anymore. Our bodies and capabilities have changed since those early years when we were in our twenties. Instead of trying to make those work today, we let them go. For us, that was not a loss. It allowed us to focus on the positions we like and enjoy. I encourage you to do the same. If you keep trying to replicate the past and get hung up on that, you'll miss out on all the amazing things that are in this season.

Dr. Kim: Do you feel you are open to trying new things in our sex life?

Nancy: Yes, you've never asked me for anything that I would consider "out there." I think I would draw the line if I was uncomfortable with it.

Dr. Kim: Oh, yes, I think you would. I think, as guys, especially when we are younger, we think of all kinds of things because, unfortunately, we let some things get in our minds that shouldn't be there.

Nancy: Yes.

Dr. Kim: When it came down to us, in our bedroom, I thought, *No, I don't think I want that to be a part of our sex life.* For me, it wasn't something that I thought was going to grow us together sexually. Maybe it might turn me on for that time, but what was that going to do for us long term? What was it going to do to you long term?

There were things that I just tossed because I didn't think they would be good for us. That doesn't mean it might not be okay for somebody else, but for us it wasn't. I've always felt like you were open and we talked about it, a new position or whatever it would be.

Questions for You:

- Husbands: What would you like your wife to consider for your sex life?
- Wives: What does it look like for you to hear your husband out and be open to trying new things?
- Wives: Do you feel like you can say no to your husband and your no will be met with love and respect? Why or why not?

- Is there anything you need to let go of when it comes to sex that you are holding on to from past seasons together?
- What new things can you enjoy right now in this current season of married sex?

3. A Husband Wants His Wife to Be Free

What does that mean? From a husband's perspective, it means for her to be free from distractions. It is pretty much a consensus that the woman's greatest sex organ is her mind. If she is free from distractions, she is able to fully engage in sex and it is enjoyable for her and her husband. Most men can make the switch in a nanosecond. A husband can be watching a game, mowing the lawn, taking a nap—it does not matter. If his wife asks, "Would you like to make love?" there is nothing that would keep him from giving her his full and undivided attention.

In talking with couples, this seems to be something that transcends the seasons of a marriage. So how do you solve this problem? First, most of you have a lot more time for the two of you alone than you had in the past. But having time alone does not automatically transport you both to the bed with your clothes off. A wife still has to think sex. She does not sit around a lot of the day thinking about making love to her husband. I talked to one woman who was truly trying to work with her husband on this. Two days a week she wrote "TS" on her calendar. What does "TS" mean? Think Sex. She was choosing to focus on sex so she could eliminate distractions.

I think that is what husbands want from their wives. I certainly do. An old anecdote illustrates this difference well: A couple is in bed and beginning to make love when the smoke alarm goes off. Smoke is streaming and there are flames down the hall. The wife says, "Let's get out of the house now!" The husband says,

"Let's finish what we started here and then call the fire department after!"

Dr. Kim: How do you free yourself from distractions when we are making love?

Nancy: When we're making love? Well, I just try to engage in the moment and get my thoughts where your thoughts are.

Dr. Kim: I don't know if you can ever do that!

Nancy: Well, just like we just said, I try to be engaged, to go with the flow, and be a participant—not just lie there!

Dr. Kim: Yes, I've seen that at times when you weren't completely there but it wasn't at a point where you said, "Hey, let's do it later on." I can just see you focus, let yourself relax, and enjoy what we're doing, and I think we both like physical touch. I think we both enjoy the physical-touch part of it, just touching each other. Instead of fighting that, I see you relaxing and trying to enjoy it.

Nancy: Yes.

Questions for You:

- What does "Think Sex" mean to you? (If this is something you want to work on, our "Think Sex Challenge" at Awesomemarriage.com was created to help you do just that! Find it under "Strengthen My Marriage" on the "Resources" drop-down.)
- Wives: How can you eliminate distractions?
- Wives: Is there anything your husband can do to help you eliminate distractions?

4. A Husband Wants His Wife to Be Willing

Here's a little-known fact: Much of a husband's pleasure in sex is simply knowing his wife wants to be with him sexually and that he can please her. Here is an example: Have you ever been in a fight with each other and your husband wants to have sex right afterward? In my experience, it seems to happen a lot. I think this is because he thinks that if his wife will have sex with him after a fight, it is a confirmation that everything is okay. One of the problems with this idea is that sex is probably the last thing on her mind after a fight.

Okay then, so what does it mean to be willing? Here are some of the men's responses: willingness, consistency, and initiative. Willingness: the way our wife responds when we initiate sex is huge for us.

I know there are times when you really do have a headache, but not always, right? This is a great issue to discuss together. Since the husband is usually the one asking, how do you make this a win for your marriage? I have counseled a number of men over the years who literally quit asking because the answer was usually no or they felt their wife was just going through the motions with a "just get this over with" attitude. Those are never good things for a marriage. Both spouses miss out in those scenarios.

So, ladies, initiate some of the time. In working with couples, the husband usually initiates most of the time. In our marriage, I have probably been the initiator 90-plus percent of the time, but the times when Nancy initiates are awesome. It answers the question, does she want to be with me? It is exciting. Your husband loves it when you initiate.

Dr. Kim: When do you like to be the initiator?

Nancy: Well, not as frequently as you, for sure. Sometimes I just want to stir things up a bit and I will then go out on a limb.

Dr. Kim: So how do you do that?

Nancy: Well, I usually start by touching you, kissing you, and rubbing your neck.

Dr. Kim: Yes, getting close to me. If we're in bed, you move close to me.

Nancy: Yes.

Dr. Kim: I think guys love when their wife initiates because usually we are the ones who initiate. I was thinking as we were getting ready to do this and it's interesting; of the different times of sex in our marriage, some of the times that really stand out to me are the ones when you initiated—just because it was just so cool.

Nancy: Something a little different.

Dr. Kim: I think it's important for wives to do that. I've worked with only one couple that I can think of where the wife really had the higher sex drive, and she did the initiating more. It seems that for most couples, it's the husband who's going to have the higher drive and initiate more often. You can talk about that as a couple. How often does it work for the wife to initiate? If it was every time, then it would not be as special.

Questions for You:

- How do you define "being willing"?
- How often do you want your wife to initiate?

5. A Husband Wants His Wife to Be Present

All of the above roll into number five. Being present is about connection, satisfaction, and taking time together afterward. Let's begin with connection. Sex is a physical, mental, emotional, and even spiritual experience. It is a mode of communication. It connects us in ways that truly are hard to describe because they are so experiential. Husbands want this with their wives. It draws men closer to them. When Nancy and I are in a regular pattern of sex, I feel closer to her. I feel more connected. It's easier for me not to be irritable. I am more motivated to serve her. I know there are a lot of factors that go into this connection but we also know that God created sex to bond a couple and to strengthen and protect a marriage. That's connection.

Now what about satisfaction? I mentioned earlier how knowing he can satisfy his wife is one of the great pleasures in sex for a man. If you are hitting on all cylinders on this in your marriage, you get a gold star today. If not, a talk is really important. As guys, we have this idea that we know everything about sex. We don't ask anyone for help or advice. The reality is that none of us are truly experts on sex and we are certainly not the expert on our wife. She is! So we need to ask her what she likes and what she does not like.

For some reason, early in marriage there was something I did during foreplay that I thought Nancy loved. Not sure where I got this idea but it was a regular part of my foreplay routine. Guys want a formula that works every time, so give us three things to do in sex that will please you and we will perform well every time. The problem is that women are more complicated than that. There's not really a "formula," or if there seems to be, it is subject to change! But I think this is actually good. It keeps sex interesting. So, about that foreplay technique that I did for years—one time after making love, I said something like, "You really like it when I do that thing, don't you?" Nancy's response? "Not really.

It's fine but there are other things I like more." Your wife is the expert on her. She is the teacher and you are the student. So talk together about what each of you likes and wants in your sex life in marriage. If you don't, you may keep doing the same thing over and over that doesn't really work instead of finding things that really do.

The last item is time together afterward. When I counsel couples, I hear about this more from wives. They say things like, "Right after sex, he jumps up and is off to something else." It's like as guys the focus problem that our wives can have before sex, we can have after. Yet, for most men, some of our closest times in our marriage have come after sex when we take the time to just lie together. You may talk or you may not. You are just being close. I know this cannot always happen after sex, but make it a priority and look for the times when it can.

In our years of marriage before kids, we often fell asleep after sex in each other's arms, still naked. I love sleeping that way with Nancy. Then when the kids were born, naked sleeping disappeared and I missed it. I would suggest it some nights but I never got a positive response. She would say, "What if the kids came in?" Finally, I said, "Can we talk about this?" I told her how I felt and I was amazed by her response. She said that she loved that too and suggested that we do that when the kids spent the night out or when we were away together. That worked for me.

Dr. Kim: If there is something in our sex life that you do not like, how would you let me know?

Nancy: I would talk to you about it, and we have done that before. I've said, "I'm not comfortable with that."

Dr. Kim: Yes. If something hurts you, I want to know. I would never try to hurt you, but I want you to tell me what is going on with your body if you are uncomfortable. The main thing is that we need to talk about it.

Nancy: Well, yes. If you don't like something, you say something.

Dr. Kim: Right and as guys, we need to learn not to take that as rejection. Take it as information that you need, and then ask your wife, "Okay, what can I do to help you with that? Is there something that we can do differently?"

Nancy: Correct. Questions, ask good questions.

Dr. Kim: How important is it to you that we are together for a while after sex?

Nancy: I love that. I think it's great.

Dr. Kim: Yes, I think it's fun when we have the time to do that. I can even remember when we've had sex in the morning sometimes and then we both fall back asleep. It's just cool that we aren't rushed. I think most of the people who are reading this, in that season of life, have those opportunities. You just want to take advantage of them.

Nancy: You bet.

Questions for You:

- How can you connect sexually?
- What is one thing your spouse can do to increase the satisfaction of sex for you?
- Wives: What do you want your husband to know about your body?
- What do you want the time after sex to look like?

What Wives Said They Want from Their Husbands

1. A Wife Wants Her Husband to Be Present

You may be thinking, *Didn't we just talk about this?* Yes, but there is a difference. The word "nails" is a good male/female example. When I say I am going to Home Depot to buy some nails, I'm not talking about the same nails that Nancy is referring to when she says she is going to get her nails done. Same word, different meanings. We have to take the time to understand what our spouse means and what they want and need from us.

When a wife wants her husband to be present during sex, it means she wants him there mentally and physically. Being present mentally means thinking only of her, being faithful to her in his mind. No intruding thoughts of other women, porn, or anything other than her. She wants to know that she turns him on and that he desires her—only her.

This is a struggle for some men. One big factor is pornography. There are two sets of statistics focused on the average age a boy first is exposed to porn. One says it's at 11 and the other says 8. For me, it was later, in my early teens. My neighborhood friend's dad had a subscription to *Playboy* magazine. The latest issue was always on the coffee table in their sitting room. One of the highlights of the month was looking through that *Playboy*. I was probably 15. Almost every man has seen some porn at some level. If you are a man and have not, consider yourself blessed. As I have said before, men are visual. What we take in visually sticks. What we have seen with porn or old girlfriends sticks. Those images are in our brains. We have to replace those with our wife. With images of her. With thoughts of her. I have prayed for many years for my sexual desire to be for Nancy and her only. God has answered that prayer.

When something is in our mind, no one knows it but us. I think that is why many men consider thoughts of unfaithfulness to be harmless. It may be true that no one else knows, but they are huge barriers in our sex lives with our wives. We are not fully embracing them. We are missing out. Plus, I think our wives have a sense when our mind is somewhere else. I can't explain it but I know it's true. So those thoughts harm the intimacy, faithfulness, and purity our married sex was meant to have. When we are not fully present mentally and physically and are not thinking of and desiring our wife only, we cheat us both out of the sex God intends for us in our marriage.

Being faithful in our minds and in our actions takes intentionality. It's not going to just happen. We have to fight for it. Two ways to help in the fight are to use accountability software on your devices and to have an accountability partner. This isn't a job for your spouse. Choose a friend who is pursuing God and purity and won't be afraid to ask the tough questions. God can—and wants to—bring you a complete victory in this battle.

Dr. Kim: Talking about distractive thoughts during sex, I thankfully haven't really had to deal with them. I've worked with people in counseling who have. Maybe it was thinking about past relationships, affairs, or pornography. Things like that get into their minds when they're having sex with their spouse. I know from talking to people who struggled with that that it can be very distracting.

If you're having sex, making love with your wife, and you're thinking about or picturing something or someone else, then you're not going to be fully present with her. Most women can pick up on that and know that you're not completely there.

I think you cheat her and you cheat yourself because you're not giving yourself totally to her. You're letting other things intrude.

I think women can let their minds drift to something besides sex but that's different from thinking about another person when they're making love with their spouse.

Nancy: Do you think men are more prone to thinking about sex in general?

Dr. Kim: Yes. I think that's why men can let in distractive thoughts of pornography, or another woman, or a past sexual experience.

Nancy: So they're sexual distractions, whereas a woman can often be thinking about what to fix for dinner or thinking about something her friends said. There are times when my mind is just not there. So you are saying that guys are more focused.

Dr. Kim: Yes, and I think that's what we talked about earlier, that the woman's greatest sex organ is her mind, because that's what you have to control.

For men, it is renewing your mind, which Paul talks about. It's replacing distractive thoughts with thoughts of your wife. Maybe you think about previous sexual experiences with your wife and those kinds of things. It allows you to be more present and to focus on the moment.

Questions for You:

- As a husband, how can you free your mind from distractions during sex?
- What practical steps can you take to refrain from porn?
- What practical steps can you take to be faithful to your spouse?

2. A Wife Wants Her Husband to Be Intimate

A lot of guys struggle to be romantic. Most of us did not have romance modeled well for us. One of the things I wish I could get every husband to embrace is that our wives need to be pursued before marriage and throughout our entire marriages. So how do you pursue her? Of course do the expected romantic things on your anniversary and Valentine's Day. But do romantic things on other days too—times when she least expects it.

Romance in the bedroom with your wife means affectionate kissing, passion for her and her body. Another part of being intimate for our wife is making sure she feels safe and comfortable with you. Think about it. In sex, your wife is very vulnerable. She is naked. You are bigger and stronger than she is. If she is going to completely give herself to you, she has to trust you. It is essential. Don't do anything that would make her fear you. If you have, tell her you are sorry and will never do that again. Ask her what would help her feel safer, more secure, and more comfortable with you, and trust her answers.

Look back at the types of intimacy we discussed in detail earlier. All of these kinds of intimacy work together to draw you closer, and that closeness is what makes sex better and better as our marriage grows over time. Pursue her through the five types of intimacy.

There you have it. You can see that being intimate with her involves more than 12 roses. As with most things with our wives, it touches the physical, the mental, and the emotional. It just takes being intentional over and over.

Dr. Kim: How do you want me to be intimate with you?

Nancy: I want you to be present with me not only physically but also mentally. I just want to be on the same level with you.

Dr. Kim: What does that mean?

Nancy: It's thinking along the same lines. Me thinking of you; you thinking of me. What can we do in this moment to make this time meaningful to both of us, pleasurable to both of us? I guess that's really the crux of it.

Dr. Kim: Do you feel safe with me?

Nancy: Oh, yes. I mean, I'm a hard person to talk to about that because I've always felt safe with you. I guess you deal with women in your practice who can be afraid or not trusting.

Dr. Kim: I counseled a couple and he was a big guy and she was a small woman but she trusted him completely. So it's not a size thing. It's feeling safe with your husband, trusting that he wouldn't do anything to hurt you, that he's going to be gentle with you and that he's going to listen if something is uncomfortable for you. I believe that's how you build trust and safety.

Nancy: In other words, a big guy needs to be conscious that she is smaller than him and he has to be conscious of making sure she's safe.

Dr. Kim: Yes, and figuring that out together. It might be that certain positions are uncomfortable for her. It is something a couple has to communicate on. I think for a guy, the only one who can judge that is his spouse. And the only one who can give me that information is you.

Nancy: Right, and people are different.

Dr. Kim: Right, what works for us may not work for someone else. We have to have those conversations. You can't take our template and put it over every marriage.

Nancy: Exactly, so you have to really communicate with each other. Talk. Tell them what turns you on and what makes you feel good, or bad, or hurts. You need to be encouraging and non-critical but really share what bothers you or what makes you feel good.

Dr. Kim: Yes, absolutely.

Questions for You:

- Wives: Is there anything that keeps you from trusting your husband in sex?
- Wives: What would make you feel safe with your husband in the bedroom? What do you need from him in order to feel safe?
- Wives: What is romantic to you?
- Husbands: How did you pursue your wife while you were dating? Are you still doing that?
- Husbands: What is one romantic thing you can do this week to pursue your wife?

3. A Wife Wants Her Husband to Be Accepting

Before Nancy and I were married, we talked about our future sex life and what we wanted it to be. From those discussions, we thought the Hollywood depictions of sex were pretty accurate. Most couples I talk to can identify with that. We were young. Our sex drives were high. We had no reason to expect this would not go on forever. But it did not, and I did not handle it well. I would do anything to convince Nancy to have sex with me whenever I wanted to, which was often. I could probably write a book on all the things *not* to do to get your wife to have sex. I found some weaknesses and played on them. But guilting or manipulating your wife will never give you the sex life that you desire.

My first step in helping us turn this around was accepting the fact that we had different sex drives. That was okay, it was normal, and it did not mean there was anything wrong with Nancy; the problem was me not accepting her. Once I accepted the difference between our sex drives, it made a huge difference. She was no longer the enemy. We could then begin working on it together as a team.

Most of the women I know fall into the comparison trap with their appearance and find fault with themselves, while they do not see the faults in others. When we take pictures, Nancy is critical of how she looks. I think women have always been critical of their looks but today's culture only makes the problem worse. We husbands can help our wives in this area by making sure to tell them how beautiful they are on a regular basis. But accepting our wives goes beyond sex drives and appearance. As husbands, part of our role is to accept our wives as they are. It is loving who they are more than loving their bodies. Women need to feel cherished for who they are. When your wife feels cherished, your intimacy will be deeper and fuller. You cannot solve the problem for her but your acceptance and love for her can go a long way toward this.

I wonder how it was for the first husband and wife, Adam and Eve, living in a perfect paradise, naked and unashamed. I guess they slept naked every night! What was their sex life like? Was it great for a time and then the differences came in? My guess is yes. I don't think God changed the blueprint over time. I think they had to deal with the same issues with sex that we do. As a man, if Nancy and I were naked together all the time—well, as good as that can sounds, I'm thankful for clothes. Adam and Eve did have a great counselor to help them work through these issues though, because God came and spent time with them every day.

My belief is that God is there for you in the same way. You may never have thought about praying for your sex life, but you can.

You can pray for wisdom, ask God to help you understand each other, and ask God to just help you grow your sex life exactly as He designed it for you. Yes, we may have different sex drives, but that is not a bad thing. It gives us something to work on together that is a significant part of our marriage.

Dr. Kim: Do you feel that I am understanding and accepting of your differences in sex?

Nancy: Yes, I do.

Dr. Kim: Okay, how do I do that?

Nancy: Well, you communicate. Don't you agree? If you think something, say something.

Dr. Kim: I think the differences are just being male or female, those kinds of things. Do you ever feel like I have not accepted that difference?

Nancy: I don't think so. I think you have grown through the years. You put a lot of your expectations on me in the early part of our marriage, but I don't think you necessarily expected me to be like you.

Dr. Kim: No. When we got married, we could have sex all the time; so early in our marriage, I thought that you had the same sex drive as I did.

Nancy: Oh, yes, that was back when you thought we could both be ready to have sex at the drop of a hat.

Dr. Kim: Yes. Then I realized that you also needed me to be caring and nurturing, and do things to help you. So then I had to figure out that, okay, we are different, instead of continuing to expect you to have the same sex drive I did all the time. I had to realize that there was more that went into it for you. I don't know; do you think I ever tried to keep you in that early marriage mold? Or do you feel like I adjusted pretty well?

Nancy: I think you adjusted pretty well.

Dr. Kim: Yes, I do too. What about accepting that we do have different sex drives? Do you think that I've done a good job of accepting that I would desire it more frequently than you would?

Nancy: Yes, I think you've come to realize that.

Dr. Kim: I'm not afraid to ask but I've learned to be okay if it's not the right time for you.

Nancy: Right.

Dr. Kim: You're good about giving an alternative.

Nancy: Right, and then, of course, some people will say a woman should never refuse her husband. How do you deal with that idea?

Dr. Kim: What do you think?

Nancy: Well, I think that if a woman, or a man, feels like they're being put upon against their will, that's going to be a struggle. It's going to cause problems. So I think both have to, once again, communicate that and say, "Let's be more open to each other's urges and also be able to accept if it's not a good time when I'm really not feeling good or I'm upset about something."

Dr. Kim: Oh, yes, I think there's responsibility for both the man and the woman, like we see in Ephesians 5. There are things that a man needs to do and things that a woman needs to do.

The idea of using Scripture to make you feel guilty about saying no to having sex, I don't see that as God's plan. God's plan is that we enjoy sex together. I think if a couple is in a situation where that's going on, that's not a healthy sex life. I think it's a man taking advantage of his wife and not loving her in the way that God would want him to. It's like she's more something to use, as opposed to someone to love, embrace, and share life with.

Nancy: I agree. I think as a woman you have to keep in mind, "How often am I saying no?" We can get in a rut where it's just more comfortable to not have sex. You're just ready to go to bed or something, and we've got to make an effort at times.

There are times when you just don't want to do it, and that's fine. But I think you don't want to get stuck there. I know I've done that in the past. I just got comfortable going to bed at a certain time, turning out the light at a certain time. I think you've got to allow a little bit of spontaneity and a little bit of, "Hey, I've not been active enough in my role."

Dr. Kim: Yes, there is responsibility both ways. But there was a time when I knew we'd be in bed and you were trying to make sure you got enough sleep, especially when you were having trouble going to sleep. If I initiated then, that really wasn't being fair to you because it would wake you up and then maybe you'd have more trouble going to sleep.

I think that was an example for me of knowing there's a time when we're in bed when I will decide I won't initiate because I know that you're already on your way to going to sleep and that sleep is important to you, and sometimes when you get woken up, you can't go back to sleep easily.

Nancy: Right, it all goes back to communicating with each other and being considerate of the other person.

Question for You:

- What do you want your husband to accept about you when it comes to sex?

4. A Wife Wants Her Husband to Be Educated

"I don't need anybody to teach me about sex. I know what to do." This is a famous line authored by many men over the years, decades, and centuries. I have thought about devising a quiz about the female body to give to these men. I think every single one of them would fail. I said it before, but your wife is the expert on her body. Your job is to get educated. When it comes to these issues, it does not seem to matter how long a couple has been married. Being in the second half of marriage does not mean we have learned all that our wives want us to learn.

We need to ask these questions: What pleases her? What are ways to help her have an orgasm? What causes her discomfort or pain? If you know the correct answers (as verified by her), you get a gold star and my congratulations. My guess is you don't. First, how much do you know about female anatomy? Can you properly identify the different parts of the vagina? Do you know what the function of each part is? Do you know what brings her the most pleasure? If you only have a grade school education on your wife's body, it's time to begin working on a PhD. Go to WebMD and learn all you can there.

The last part of this is giving her the freedom to express pleasure without judgment. Our wives can be inhibited here. Maybe they were raised with the idea that sex is bad or wrong or dirty. Well-meaning parents do well-meaning things to help keep their daughters pure until marriage. The problem with that is that it does much more harm than good. They may enter marriage with their virginity intact but be left with a distorted view of sex. There is not a switch to flip on your wedding night that changes her from "don't do it" to "do it and enjoy it." Every wife needs to know that she can express her pleasure in sex without judgment. I think that is really what we want as husbands. If she is expressing pleasure, you have succeeded as her husband. So be educated. It is not too late and she will love you for it! Learn about female anatomy. Learn about her anatomy. Learn what helps her achieve orgasm. Let her orgasm first. Encourage her to express pleasure.

Dr. Kim: How good have I been at knowing your body and what you like and do not like? Where could I do better?

Nancy: Well, you get an A+. Don't you think most guys really do get it?

Dr. Kim: Yes, but guys think, *Okay, I should be able to grab my wife's breasts whenever I want to,* and for some women that might not be a turn-on at all. We have to realize that we need to be gentle with our wives. I've learned that's important to you, and if we're going to have good sex, it works much better when I do the things that work for you.

Nancy: Well, it's all trial and error, especially when starting out. Once again, it's communication. Tell them, "Hey, that hurts," or "That really isn't what turns me on; try this." You've got to communicate.

Dr. Kim: You have never really had a problem having an orgasm, but for some women that is a problem or it takes them longer. The guy has to know what he can do to help his wife have an orgasm. Ask her, "Is there something that needs to happen?" "Do I need to make sure you have an orgasm before I do?" Ask questions like that. Sex is not a selfish thing. The idea is for both spouses to be pleased.

Nancy: Well, once again, you don't have to pay a counselor to figure this out.

Dr. Kim: No. For couples that are in this stage of marriage, if you haven't done some of these things well in the past, it's not too late. It's time for you to sit down and have that talk about your bodies, what you like, or what you don't like. It's never too late to do that.

I think even as we age, maybe something that was a part of our sex life at one point isn't anymore. Maybe now it's uncomfortable or it's not as pleasing as it was at one time. So it's a work in progress your entire marriage.

Nancy: Right. Coming into the second part of your life, it's a good time to start over. If you don't like the way things have been, start the conversation. "Let's start this whole process over and learn each other like our relationship is brand new." Put a second life into your second part of life.

Dr. Kim: That's really good. In premarital counseling, when I talk with a couple about their sexual relationship, I tell them that this is a learning experience, so they've got to communicate things that they've been thinking. No matter what stage you are in, if you find yourselves struggling in this area, you can redefine it. You can really work on that together, and talk about it, and experiment together.

Maybe one of you says, "I'd like to try this position." The other says, "Okay." And so you try it and then afterward you talk about it and you say, "That was great. Why haven't we been doing that?" or "Nah, let's try something different." And you continue to work on it.

Do you feel I could have done better in this area with you?

Nancy: I guess the hardest thing for you was learning that I didn't want to be as active as you did sexually, and I think you've grasped that.

Dr. Kim: It took me a while. Part of that was being young and having a really high sex drive at that point.

Nancy: We were young and we both had stronger sex drives. Now it's not about the lust; it's about the love, the *dod.* It's just different and I think it's better. Even though it might not be as frequent, it is better.

Dr. Kim: Yes, I agree. I think *dod* is a great word because it's a mingling of souls, which sex really is. You're just caught up with each other.

Nancy: I don't know how to describe it completely. It's a deep emotional and spiritual level.

Questions for You:

- Husbands: How well do you know your wife's anatomy?
- Wives: What do you want your husband to know more about?

5. A Wife Wants Her Husband to Be Adventurous

Honestly, this one surprised me. I wondered if this was the same thing that husbands were saying with "be open." The women's comments said they wanted to try new things. They don't want to get into a rut. Something different from the missionary position.

It seems the most common sex position is the missionary position, where the couple is face to face with the woman on the bottom and the man on the top. I always wondered how that position got that name, so I finally researched it. It seems that early European missionaries discovered that many of the native people they encountered were into all kinds of different sexual positions. The shocked missionaries declared that only the couple facing, man-on-top position was acceptable before the Lord. My problem with that claim is the Bible. Their declaration does not line up what we see in the Song of Solomon. My take is this: God gives us a lot of leeway in what we can do in our sexual relationship in marriage. There is not a good list or a bad list.

So that's the legend of the missionary position. If that is your favorite position, it's perfectly okay. It works well and seems to have always been a common sexual position in most of the world.

I think what the women are telling us here is that they are fine with trying new positions or places or whatever that the two of you want to do. For most couples, they settle into two or three positions that they enjoy that work for them. My suggestion would be to try new ones from time to time. Do some research together or come up with your own ideas. In counseling, I tell couples that if they both agree to it and it is not harmful to either and not against the law, go for it. *The Celebration of Sex* manual by Dr. Douglas E. Rosenau is full of drawings illustrating different positions. Nancy and I have had this book since it came out in 2002. Probably enough said on that!

One other very important thing: sex should be fun! Someone said sex is the most fun a couple can have together without laughing and there are also times we laugh. Nancy and I have learned to do that. If we try something new and it is not working, instead of getting frustrated with each other, we laugh. It may interrupt the sex for a few minutes, but laughing together may be a natural response at times, and it's another great way to connect.

Another big thing wives want is for us to be creative in how we please them. Being adventurous with foreplay is what a lot of women want—finding new ways to please her. If it's too robotic, it can take the enjoyment out of it for women.

One other thing that can be adventurous is to change the place you make love. I love our bed and I love having sex in our bed, but why not venture out? Have sex in a different place in your home. The shower or bathtub is a great option. On a blanket in front of the fireplace. I even had one couple that got in the backseat of their car in the garage. Have fun with this. Both of you can suggest new positions or places. Make your sex life a team project for you two. Bottom line: Be adventurous; get out of the rut.

Dr. Kim: How adventurous have we been in sex? What does that mean to you today?

Nancy: I'm always open. I think we're comfortable where we are right now but if we ever feel we're in a rut again, I'm open.

Dr. Kim: Yes, and we vary some things. We try not to be in a rut. I think there are certain positions that we found over the years that are more comfortable or more exciting for us.

Nancy: Oh, yes.

Dr. Kim: We all tend to stick with some of those but I think it's good for every couple to have at least two or three different positions that they work on together. If you can, if physically you can do that, just add some variety in and then be creative with it. I remember when the book *The Celebration of Sex* came out and I brought it home and the kids were still home. We had to hide it somewhere as we didn't want the kids finding it. Sometimes we need a jump start. Sometimes you look at a book like that together and you think, *Well, this might be something that would really be fun for us, something that we would enjoy.* I think we've been pretty good about that; if one of us comes up with an idea, we are open to it and talk about it.

Nancy: Exactly.

Question for You:

- What does being adventurous in sex mean to you?

So What Does Your Spouse Want?

We have looked at what husbands want from their wives and what wives want from their husbands. Now you have a look inside what your spouse wants from you. What's your next step? My suggestion would be for each of you to take the lists above—husbands take the list of what you want from your wife, and wives take the list of what you want from your husband.

Rank each item from 1 to 5 with 1 being the most important to you. Now take the number 1 from each list, share that with each other, talk about it together, and then begin to implement what you have learned into your marriage. Is there something you would add or take away from the list? Talk about it. Share what's really important to you, what you hope for, and how you can work together to achieve it. As you feel you have your 1s, go to the 2s, and then on down your list until you have worked through all 5. Take your time on each. Don't rush. You can cycle through them again from time to time.

The goal is to get the conversation started and to become more intentional about working together on having all God intends for you in your sex life. By focusing on each other and being intentional day after day, your sex life in your marriage will go from where it is today to . . . well, the sky really is the limit.

Final Thoughts

Love, intimacy, and sex. Which area needs the most work in your marriage? What do you need to do individually and together to be intentional about growing that area of your marriage? All three are important and I believe you can work on all of them at the same time. They really do go together. Learning to love better and love more definitely affects intimacy and sex. As you learn to be more intimate, your love for each other and your sexual relationship will grow. As you learn how to improve your sex life, your love and your intimacy will grow.

Think about it this way: love, intimacy, and sex are three pieces of a puzzle. Each piece alone is important, but when you fit the three pieces together, you get the complete picture. You have a picture of marriage the way God designed it to be.

Now it's the second half of your marriage. You have the ball and an open field in front of you. It is your choice. You can do nothing and reminisce about the first half of your marriage, or you can get in the game. You can make this season of your marriage something that you both cherish and enjoy.

Some of you are in a better place with your marriage today than others. Wherever you are now, it's okay. Where your marriage is today does not matter as much as where it will be tomorrow, next month, next year, and hopefully a lot of years after that. The way you live out your second half of marriage can impact not just the two of you but also your family and those around you.

I want your marriage to be everything God designed it to be. He has an incredible plan for your marriage and that does not change in the second half. You can embrace it or not, but if you choose to embrace it, you will score a lot of touchdowns in the second half.

We would love to hear your story and how this book has impacted you and your marriage. My email address is drkim@awesome-marriage.com and Nancy's is nancykimberling@me.com. Thank you for letting us share our story with you.